HOW
YOU
LIVE

HOW YOU LIVE

LESSONS LEARNED *from*
POINT OF GRACE

B&H
PUBLISHING
NASHVILLE, TENNESSEE

Copyright © 2020 by Point of Grace
All rights reserved.
Printed in China

978-1-5359-8473-7

Published by B&H Publishing Group
Nashville, Tennessee

Dewey Decimal Classification: 248.84
Subject Heading: CHRISTIAN LIFE / LIFE SKILLS / QUALITY OF LIFE

Point of Grace lifestyle photography by Cole Gorman/Wander Creative Productions.
Wardrobe styling by Amber Lehman and Beth Lehman/Jandy Works. Hair and makeup styling by
Carol Maxwell and Kara Gaylor. Family photos by McPeak Photography and Kelley Tansil.
Floral patterns and elements by Laras Wonderland/Creative Market. Stock photos and
vectors by WindAwake, Africa Studio (p 2), Billion Photos (p 12), Silver Wolf (p 38), Lamiquela
(p 43), MyImages - Micha (p 48), Peshkova (p 58), MicrostockStudio (p 76), fongbeerredhot
(p 84), and Evgeny Karandaev (p 101) /shutterstock. Stock photos by Silvrshootr (p 104),
Customdesigner (p 116), and Alice Rodnova (p 124) /istock. Stock photo by LisaTherese
(p 148) /unsplash. Stock photo by THAIS VARELA (p 16) /stocksy. Tabletop photography by
Randy Hughes. Doodle illustrations and hand lettering by Kristi Smith, Juicebox Designs LLC.

1 2 3 4 5 6 7 • 24 23 22 21 20

Shelley Breen

On a cool spring day in 1969, Shelley Phillips was born to Joe and Sharon Phillips at the U.S. Air Force Base in Belleville, Illinois.

Only a few weeks later, Joe boarded his military transport for a tour of duty in Korea. He often shares a story of the overwhelming emotion he felt waving good-bye to his six-week-old daughter, Shelley, as he departed.

A few years later, after Joe's return from service and a relocation to Arkansas, the family was blessed with another baby girl, Shelley's younger sister Robyn. As the years passed, seventh grade ended up being a pivotal school year for Shelley as she, with the encouragement of her choral teacher, discovered her deep love and passion for music.

Olivia Newton John's "I Honestly Love You" was her first vocal solo, and she was hooked. Church choral groups and vocal ensembles became her mainstay in the coming years. A special gift from her mom, Amy Grant's classic *Age to Age* album, ignited an even deeper passion in Shelley to share songs of faith and inspiration. There was rarely a time when Shelley missed a Sandi Patty or Michael W. Smith concert when they came to town, which propelled her love for vocal stage performance.

Receiving the prestigious Presidential Scholarship enabled Shelley to attend Ouachita Baptist University in Arkansas. She could be found participating in all of the school's choral groups she could find: the Praise Singers, Ouachitones, and University Chorus among many others. Her studies resulted in a Bachelor of Arts degree in Vocal Performance.

During this time in college, Shelley joined musical forces with a few like-minded girls, including her roommate, Denise Jones. Along with others, they formed a quartet that evolved from performing at simple Summer Outreach concerts and camps, to being discovered at Estes Park's Talent Search in the Rockies, to making musical history. The group Point of Grace was born, and more than twenty-five years later, it remains one of the most influential vocal groups in Contemporary Christian Music.

In the early 1990s, Shelley and the Point of Grace members moved to Tennessee, where she eventually met her future husband, David Breen, at a business meeting on Music Row. Their daughter, Caroline, joyfully came into their lives in 2002. Shelley and her family continue to make Tennessee their home. ◆

Denise Jones

In 2018, Point of Grace was inducted into the Oklahoma Music Hall of Fame—an especially high and cherished honor for founding group member and native "Okie," Denise Masters.

Denise was born in Norman, Oklahoma, to Don and Janice. At the tender age of three, she stood on a weathered wooden choir bench at her grandpa's church and sang her first solo, "Jesus Loves Me." This moment began a love for music that would take her on an unforgettable journey.

With faith and family as crucial components in her upbringing, Denise glows with fond memories of her parents and two older sisters, often sharing "Sunday Specials" from the platform. In fact, on many occasions her extended family gathered around the piano with guitars, fiddles, banjos, and any instruments they could get their hands on, singing Gospel, Bluegrass, and Country music.

Throughout middle and high school, Denise participated in every shape and size of choral opportunity. This involvement prompted her church music director to encourage her to further her passions with a college degree in music.

And further her passions she did. Ouachita Baptist University in Arkansas was the place where Denise truly blossomed as an artist. As a Ouachita singer, Tiger Tunes Hostess, Ouachitone, and even lead actor in the musical *Oklahoma*, she thrived in the arts.

During her college years, Denise and roommate Shelley Phillips joined forces with a couple other dear friends to form what was to become one of the greatest vocal groups in Christian music: multi-award winners Point of Grace.

Denise's various contributions to the group cannot be understated. A tireless work ethic, and equally sweet spirit have made this woman a driving force in all of her pursuits.

While taking summer classes back in Oklahoma to complete her Bachelors in Music Education degree, Denise found her soulmate, Stu Jones. The two would become the first married couple in Point of Grace. They were blessed with two boys, Spence and Price, who currently attend The University of Oklahoma. Although the family has resided in Nashville for almost three decades, Denise is quick to acknowledge that they are all "Sooners for Life"! ◆

Leigh Cappillino

Born in the foothills of South Carolina, Leigh Darby fell in love with music at an early age. Her love of music was inspired by her parents, especially her mom, Robin, the church pianist and Youth Choir director.

Leigh's college education included a minor in Vocal Performance from Anderson College and a major in religion from Charleston Southern University.

In her early twenties, Leigh saw her musical abilities lead to opportunities as a member of the prestigious vocal group Truth, where she met her future husband, Truth guitarist Dana Cappillino.

The mid-1990s would bring one of the most enriching seasons of Leigh's life as she became the worship leader for all of the national conferences created by the ground-breaking Women of Faith ministry. Under the tutelage of some of the world's greatest Christian leaders, Leigh's faith journey and heart for people grew by leaps and bounds.

In 2002, a joyful addition came to Leigh's family—a precious baby girl named Darby Mae. Soon after, the members of Point of Grace invited Leigh to be a part of their esteemed musical family.

More than fifteen years have gone by since first joining Point of Grace, and in every step of the journey, Leigh has experienced the incredible blessing of being in this trio. Year by year, they continue to grow as close friends, award-winning musicians, and authors.

And as it turns out, the Point of Grace group isn't the only family that has grown over time! Most recently, Leigh's family was made complete with the addition of Andrew Lincoln Cappillino, a heavenly surprise after twenty years of marriage. ◆

CONTENTS

HELLO FRIEND

No matter the situation, experience, or transition we go through in life, one thing is certain: we all learn lessons along the way. Seasons change, and hopefully, as we grow and learn, we change with them.

For you, perhaps the season right now is one of beginnings—a new job, a new school, a new baby, or a new home might be on the horizon. Or, maybe your current season is one of reflection, as you think on your marriage, your parenting, your struggles, your work, or your friendships. Perhaps, instead, it's a period of endings you find yourself in—soaking up the final days with a child about to head to college, closing the chapter to a job you've had for years, or saying good-bye to a beloved community as you move to another city.

Or, maybe this book isn't in your hands for you at all, but for someone else. Perhaps you have a loved one in mind—someone who is approaching a certain event, season, or change in life that you want to commemorate. Maybe you simply want a way to say, "We've all braved this kind of thing before, in some way or another, and we've all come out on the other side of it with valuable lessons learned. You are not alone."

Now, we don't pretend to have all the wisdom or knowledge or answers in the world. There's no way we could. Truth be told, we've gotten life wrong a lot more times than we've gotten it right! But through it all—the ups and the downs, the seasons on the road and at home, the failures and the successes—God has taught us some things along the way, and we can't thank Him enough for it.

As you read through this book, our prayer is this: that you'd look beyond the lessons we've learned in various seasons of life, toward the One who taught them to us. No matter what you face, no matter who you might be trying to walk beside right now as *they* brave the next few steps in their journey, no matter what the particular season of life may be, God will meet you, keep you, and teach you. Whether you learn it the hard way or the easy way, He will *always* be exactly what you need.

And the best part? The back of this book offers a tangible way for you to move beyond our stories and record what really matters: your own lessons learned. Use this as a dedicated place to document what God has taught you over the years, so you can remind yourself of His great grace in the future, or perhaps even pass on these insights as a gift to a loved one who might need your wisdom right about now.

With love,

Denise, Leigh, and Shelley

> Our prayer is this: that you'd look beyond the lessons we've learned in various seasons of life, toward the One who taught them to us. . . . He will *always* be exactly what you need.

CONSISTENCY

Have you ever had a moment so impactful, that even though it happened long ago, you can remember every detail in your mind's eye?

It was probably 1992—as Point of Grace was just ramping up—that we spent a lot of time in the city of Houston. A man named Steve Seelig was the singles pastor at First Baptist Church there, and he was working hard on our behalf to make sure the entire world knew about us and our music. We loved Steve with all our hearts; he was a true fan from day one, who eventually became our first booking agent, and ultimately a father figure to us. He introduced us to a wonderful woman from the church who was teaching Sunday school and also beginning her own speaking and teaching ministry for women. Her name was Beth Moore.

Even in Beth's beginnings as a women's Bible teacher, she was so full of wisdom, and you naturally wanted to push the godly insights she gleaned from the Word straight into your soul. I remember so vividly sitting down in Steve's office with Beth one hot Houston day to talk about where things were headed with our group. She told us we were no doubt on the brink of beginning a long career in Christian music. I'll never forget Beth looking us straight in the eye and asking, "What do you want people to say about you when your ministry is complete?"

We all had trouble figuring out what to say—*is there even a right answer*, we wondered? After we stumbled around for a bit, Beth prodded us in the right direction: "I think the greatest thing you will want to be said of you is that you were

faithful." Truer words were never spoken, and I remember thinking that on one hand that sounded so simple, but being faithful to the Lord's work would come to hold so many complexities throughout our career. In the end, that's exactly what each of us wanted to be said of us and our ministry—that we were "steadfast, immovable, always excelling in the Lord's work," as 1 Corinthians 15:58 puts it.

Faithful. Steadfast. Excelling. I think these culminate in the word *consistency*. Whether we are on tour, in our homes, or making everyday little decisions, we wanted to be consistently faithful to do the next right thing that came our way. While we certainly stumble every day, we are ever-aiming to be women who consistently get back up and walk in the faithful direction. We want to know and live out a secret truth: small but consistent and faithful decisions we make to the glory of God over the long haul are the ultimate freedom! Consistency, as it turns out, is the abundant and good life. That's been true for us over the course of our ministry, and it's true for you too. ◆

"Years ago, as new parents, my husband and I were visiting some friends who had a son who was probably three. After a long day of playing, his mother told David to go and take a bath. There was no screaming, yelling, kicking, or crying. David immediately got up from the floor and went to take a bath. She only asked him once. I was stunned, and as a new mother I asked her, 'How did you get him to do that? How did you get him to take a bath without a fight?' His mother shared her secret. Consistency. She said, 'I knew I needed to be consistent in everything I asked him to do, and follow through with discipline if needed. It only took a few times for him to realize who was lovingly the boss.' My husband and I followed our friends' example of being consistent as parents, and that rewarded us with many happy days with our kids. We enjoyed every minute, every age, and every phase of life with our kids. They were a joy . . . and that made us joyful!"

BONITA SEELIG
wife of Steve, mother, and good friend

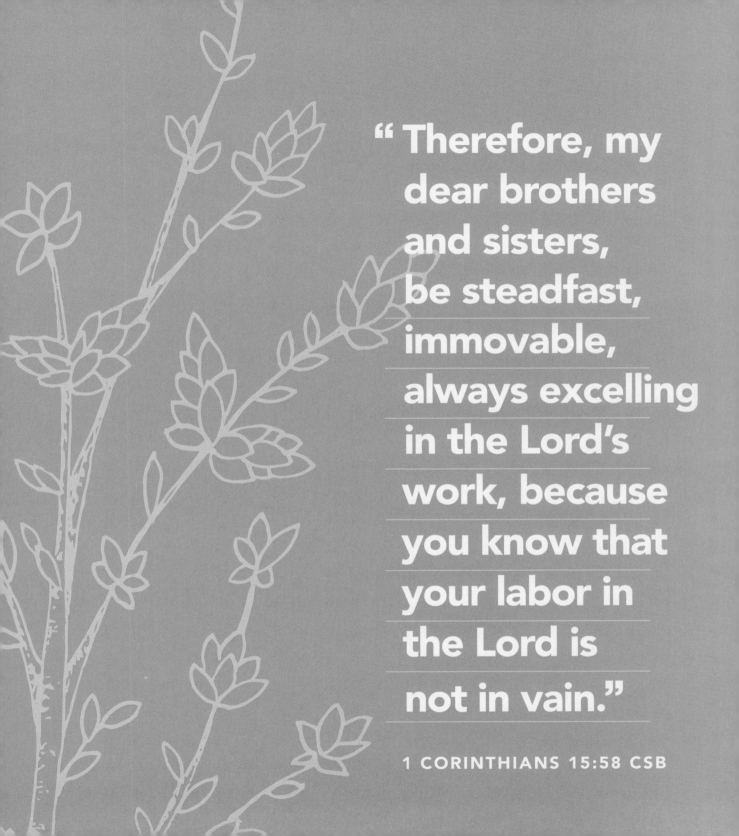

"Therefore, my dear brothers and sisters, be steadfast, immovable, always excelling in the Lord's work, because you know that your labor in the Lord is not in vain."

1 CORINTHIANS 15:58 CSB

GOD'S TONE OF VOICE

My youngest son informed me the other day that I have rude "texting etiquette." I had no idea what he was talking about. Apparently, when you put a period at the end of the word, the receiver assumes you are saying something with a sarcastic tone. For example:

> **Price:** *Hey Mom, I'm going to stop by Sonic on my way home.*

> **Me:** *Okay.*

See, when I read that text, I think I was simply saying "Alright. Sounds great." But to Price? In his mind, my text reads this way instead: "*Sigh.* *Okay,* if you HAVE to." He read my words and assumed I was frustrated by ending the whole ordeal with, you know, a period.

Again, I had no intention of saying it that way. I was just saying, "Okay." I might have been in the middle of something that didn't allow for the extra smiley face, thumbs up, or "thanks for letting me know!"

This texting debacle sent me into deep thought. *OH DEAR . . . How many other people have I been rude to over texts because I had no idea of the rules?*

The sad part is I would love it if my children automatically assumed my tone would be sweet because that's what they are used to hearing. But to be honest, sometimes it's not. I get why they can wonder which sort of tone is showing up in their messages back and forth to me.

Tone of voice can mean everything. Thankfully, God's tone of voice has changed in my head over the past few years, and it has altered my way of hearing Him as I pray and read His Word.

For example, His promise in Psalm 32:8 says this: "I will instruct you and show you the way to go; with my eye on you." Like Price, I used to hear it the wrong way, and interpreted it as: "I'm telling you where to go and *watch out, because I'm watching you* (with a stern eye) to make sure you do what I tell you!"

Really, the tone behind God's promise here is this: "I love you so much. I'm going to help you by showing you the best path for your life and I'll always be watching over you. You will never walk this path alone. My eye has not shifted elsewhere. I see you and I care and I will lead you."

There are countless verses I used to read the wrong way because I didn't understand God's tone toward me was *loving*. This doesn't mean that God can't give us stern correction, but it does mean that His communication with us *always* flows out of love. Sometimes I didn't read His Word that way, and it kept me distant and afraid. Now that I remember His tone of voice is based in love, I'm warm and receptive to His instruction. And you can be too! ◆

What type of tone do I hear when God speaks to me through His Word or Spirit?

Why do I often interpret His tone this way?

What Scripture passages can I cling to that assure me that His tone toward me is always based in love?

"GOD'S COMMUNICATION WITH US ALWAYS FLOWS OUT OF LOVE."

HOPES
AND
DREAMS

I've been singing in church as far back as I can remember. My mother was my choir teacher all the way up to my college years. Mom encouraged me at a *very* early age that I had a special gift for singing.

College gave me the confidence of what I wanted to do for the rest of my life—SING! I gained so much experience and appreciated all styles of music. Those years I was like a musical sponge. I immersed myself in music, traveling every weekend performing with a live band. This experience became the driving force of my hopes and dreams.

My college years led to yet another leg of the journey, when I joined the musical group Truth as a vocalist through the encouragement and recommendation of my college ensemble director, Dr. Rick Brewer. My time in Truth eventually led to industry-wide relationships, not to mention the introduction to my husband!

New opportunities came from my time in Truth, which over time, amounted to four different singing groups, more than thirty albums recorded, traveling the globe, and who knows how many shows. I still pinch myself in amazement as I celebrate more than fifteen years with Point of Grace.

My hopes and dreams started as a young girl. Along the way, others like my mom and my ensemble director noticed and encouraged me toward the ways God had gifted me. I think this is a very important element when it comes to the hopes and dreams that we see in the hearts of others around us. Taking the time to notice and encourage others in their gifting can help them identify what God might be planning for their lives and give them courage to pursue it.

Your hopes, dreams, and passions shouldn't be your identity at the end of the day, but they shouldn't be shunned either. Don't underestimate the desires God has placed within you. Ask God to help define and refine them. Ask Him to help you let go of dreams that aren't really good for you and to take hold of dreams that are exactly what He's calling you to. Ask Him to bring people into the process to encourage you and show you the way. Trust God with the dream you have, speak encouragement over the gifts He has given to others, and watch Him move in your life. ◆

"My mom has always emphasized the importance of following my dreams and passions since I was a little girl. She is a beautiful example of using the passion and gifts God gave her to advance the kingdom of God. I have learned that using your gifts for the glory of Jesus has an impact beyond anything you will ever do. I'm grateful and so blessed . . . and strive to follow in the footsteps of my mom; she is my biggest cheerleader and my encouragement!"

DARBY CAPPILLINO
my daughter, age sixteen

"Trust God with the dream you have, speak encouragement over the gifts He has given to others, and watch Him move in your life."

What has God taught you about your own hopes and dreams?

What advice would you give to someone else who is fighting to trust God with theirs?

FEAR OF FAILURE

When I look back on my high school experience, there is one thing that stands out to me more than anything else: I was flat-out terrified of failure. From making myself literally sick over making good grades, to not taking chances when I should have, most of my decisions were based on the fear of failing.

One particular memory stands out in my mind. Given my involvement in my church choir and also choir at school, I was singing a lot by the time I was in the 9th grade. My high school choir director was so encouraging, and I finally felt like I had found something that I enjoyed and was good at. Try-outs for the high school musical rolled around, and they were doing *Grease*. I loved the music from that movie and had the double LP album that I would sing obsessively along with every night in my mirror.

I knew the music like the back of my hand—but every time I went to sign up for try-outs, I just couldn't do it. I was so afraid of failing—so afraid of not being offered a part. So I never did it. I never even tried out. In a school where I was known as "the singer" by my classmates, I couldn't muster up

the tiniest bit of courage to risk failure! It's wild to think that a professional singer would be so cow-ardly in her younger years, but I was. Now when I look back, it's almost laughable.

I see it so clearly now—how fear of not measuring up can keep some of life's greatest experiences from you.

So I have tried at every turn to encourage my own daughter to go for it every single time. And I'm so proud of her when she puts herself out there—especially in the times when she fails. I know that sounds odd, but it couldn't be more true. It says so much about her character and resilience to lose gracefully and keep her perspective and persistence. Anyone can be proud of their daughter when risk leads to success. But my momma's heart beams

In what area of life do you most fear the possibility of failure? Why?

What would look different about your life if you believed God truly held all the chips?

Is God leading you to take a chance on something right now? To put yourself out there, try, and trust Him with the results?

What is it?

even brighter when she risks and falls down, only to get back up, keep moving forward, and trust the Lord all over again the next go-around. Resilience is the real success!

If I had a dime for every time I have told Caroline, "Do your best and then let the chips fall," I would be rich. And in all seriousness, I believe in that little catchphrase with all my heart, because God holds all the chips. He has our best interest at heart. He will "place the chips" or let them fall where they need to be. Sometimes it will be on the side of failure, sometime success, as the world defines them. But in each case, the real win is in trusting Him no matter what.

There are so many reasons not to take a chance on something in this life, but fear of failure should not be one of them. ◆

"I believe that whenever I 'fail' it makes me stronger and causes me to learn something. God allows failure to happen because He knows that it will teach us more about ourselves and Him in the end; this is something that my parents have always taught me."

CAROLINE BREEN
my daughter, age seventeen

"Do your best and then let the chips fall, because **God holds all the chips.**"

PRIORITIES, ROUTINES, AND RHYTHMS

The Point of Grace girls and I get this question so often: "How do you juggle life and also do what you do?"

Let me start by saying that I don't get it right every day. But for the most part, if I stick to what I call my "foundational commitment," I have a better chance. The foundational commitment for me is a rhythm of routine and priorities that incorporates the top three things I consider most important. If these three things are part of my day, I consider it a day fulfilled and successful. For me, those three things are prayer with Bible study, thirty minutes of exercise, and a healthy meal with family around the table. This establishes mental peace in order to conquer the day ahead and requires approximately one to two hours, depending on my schedule for the week. If I can make good on that foundational commitment, I feel balanced and faithful to the things that matter in life.

Yes, life can be unpredictable and sometimes wiggle room is necessary for miscellaneous detours, family emergencies, meetings, and so on. However, having daily priorities creates a rhythm for your life.

If you are trying to juggle too many things, those things will begin to overtake your life and then you are left frustrated and extremely tired. Instead, choose the reverse. Fight to squeeze as much out of life as you can instead of letting *it* squeeze the life out of *you*! This requires you to simplify your priorities and commit to a few things that matter most.

What are those three things for you? That might depend on what season of life you are in. A newlywed, a new mom, a single professional woman, a widow, maybe caring for a sick family member or friend. Whatever the season, we have to be intentional about nurturing ourselves and simplifying our endless commitments so that we can actually be *consistently faithful* to the few God has actually called us to. This process is not a selfish one. Instead it allows us to be better for those that need us in each capacity. It helps us bring our most healthy self to others in service.

As the famous saying goes, "Every day you should have something to do, someone to love, and something to look forward to!" Priorities. Rhythms. Foundational commitments. Whatever you want to call them, take the time with God to ponder what He says yours should be, and then live by them. ◆

COWBOY CAVIAR

This recipe is one of my family's favorite snacks, and it's also super healthy! Thanks to Dana's aunt, Donna, for passing this down.

Serves 6–8

CAVIAR

2 avocados cut into cubes

1 diced tomato

11 ounce can of shoe peg corn (or petite white corn), drained

15 ounce can of black-eyed peas, drained and rinsed

2/3 cup fresh cilantro (leaves only), chopped

3 green onions, chopped

DRESSING

1 cup olive oil

1/4 cup red wine vinegar

2 cloves garlic, minced

1/2 teaspoons cumin

splash of lemon juice

3/4 teaspoon salt

1/8 teaspoon black pepper

1 teaspoon Worcestershire sauce

hot sauce, to taste

INSTRUCTIONS

1. Combine all caviar ingredients in a bowl. Set aside.
2. Combine all dressing ingredients in a separate bowl.
3. Add the dressing ingredients mixture to the caviar ingredients mixture.
4. Stir and chill for at least two hours.
5. Serve with your favorite tortilla chips.

"SIMPLIFYING
OUR ENDLESS COMMITMENTS LETS US BE CONSISTENTLY FAITHFUL TO THE FEW GOD HAS ACTUALLY CALLED US TO."

ESTABLISHING HEALTHY PRIORITIES AND RHYTHMS

In today's society, the best advice I can give is this:

Release yourself from your social media feeds and other forms of online distractions at least one day a week. Call it your "Sabbath" if you need to. Then pay close attention to how much actual face time you now have to offer others in your sphere of life!

COMPARISON

It's no surprise that most women struggle with the problem of comparing themselves to each other. Why? Because it's one of the slyest ways in which the enemy steals our joy and keeps us from doing the unique things that God created us to do for His glory.

And it's not just the enemy who tempts us to doubt that we're made for a specific purpose and design. You and I are also to blame. Boiled down, the root issue with comparison is sin. God says so many times in Scripture that we aren't to covet what others have. I don't know about you, but I have certainly coveted the gifts that God has given others. Shelley has a gift for hospitality, Leigh has a gift for organization, another friend always seems to know the right thing to say in any situation, while someone else can sing circles around me. Not that we can't learn things from others, but when my focus is to try and mold myself into their image instead of Christ's image, I am the one who loses myself in the midst of it all. Trying to be like someone else has not only sucked the joy out of my life, but it has caused me to get depressed and even jealous of the good that happens in the lives of others. It's ugly!

"Stay in your lane"—every time I hear this well-known phrase, I laugh a little. There's so much truth to the statement. God has created a lane for us all—a path He wants us on. But when we cross into someone else's lane, there is always some sort of wreck. If I'm so focused on the car next to me because it seems prettier, classier, cooler, or whatever, instead of the road God has put in front of *me*, I'll miss the very wonderful and exciting journey God has planned personally for my life, not to mention the lives He wants me to minister to.

With comparison, the biggest lesson I can hand down is found in 1 Peter 4:10: "Each of you should use whatever gift you have received to serve others . . ." (NIV). Use the gifts God has specifically given you to serve others, knowing that God's gifts to each person is varied. And that's a good thing or else both you and I would be redundant in this world! And in the end, we are all trying to look like *Jesus* instead of someone else anyway! ◆

Who do you compare yourself to the most?

What sorts of things amplify your comparison struggle—maybe social media or something else?

What are some Scripture promises you can claim to fight this battle well?

What habits might you need to step away from in order to limit the hold comparison has on you?

"A few years back, my pastor said, 'Nothing destroys contentment like comparison.' I realize that when I compare myself to others, it's always a losing game, but when I live with a heart of gratitude for the blessings and opportunities I've been given, I am overwhelmed by God's goodness to me."

TERRI WOOD
friend, mentor, wife, and mom of four girls

"We're all trying to look like Jesus, not someone else."

INTEGRITY

In my own process of sanctification, a major way God has developed me in the integrity department is through my spouse, David. If anyone is the living embodiment of all that the book of Proverbs tells us about integrity (outside of Jesus, of course), it would be him. He has probably taught me more about integrity than any person I know.

I always joke with people that "I'm the mean one and he's the nice one in our marriage." Opposites attract, right? Usually I'm joking, but unfortunately for me (and him!), there is some truth behind that statement. I rejoice that God has opened my eyes to a lot of my sin over the years, but I still have a long way to go.

David has been rock-solid, and rarely ever wavering, in his almost seemingly natural bent to just plain 'ol *do right*. Now I know it's not "natural" for any of us to do right outside of God's spirit, but you get my point. His integrity is consistent—and I believe for you to claim yourself as an honorable person, consistency is key.

David is in the music business, so early in our marriage I began to get an up close look at the inner workings of booking agencies, record labels, and the like.

As an artist, I had a different perspective. Everyone I met in the industry was always super nice, and honestly, on their best behavior around our group. But that's not always how it is on a daily basis behind the closed doors of any given office.

I can remember times over the years that David would come home and tell me about a conflict he had, and I would immediately start fuming. Whether it was an artist who betrayed him, a coworker unfairly jockeying for position, or a promoter or agent that had lied to him—whatever it was—I would go into "Well, how are you going to fight back?" mode. And I can tell you that time, after time, after time, *after time* I watched David accept the circumstances with grace, rarely even uttering a harsh word about the other guy, and reassuring me that it would all work out in the end. He's certainly had his moments of anger and standing up for himself when it was required, but they have always been the exception, not the norm. Overall, I have seen him countless times walk into a room and sincerely shake the hand and greet someone that I would have turned my nose up to or ignored because of something they had done to me. But that's just not David's style, and thankfully, it's not really mine anymore either.

David's always had this consistency, this absolute and utter resolve that God will take care of him and our family. Because of his example, I have come so far in my own reactions toward people who wrong me just by watching his consistent integrity in the music business. It's the daily decisions and reactions that a person's reputation is eventually made of, and it's never too late to start. ◆

Who is a "David" in your own life—someone who has wonderful and consistent integrity? How can you tell?

In what area are you most tempted to compromise your integrity? Why?

What promises can you cling to from the Lord when you are tempted to cut corners or waver in your godliness?

What lessons has God taught you about integrity over the years? What piece of advice would you pass on to others regarding integrity?

"TO DO WHAT IS RIGHT AND JUST IS MORE ACCEPTABLE TO THE LORD THAN SACRIFICE."

PROVERBS 21:3 ISV

CONFLICT

Most conflict erupts when we refuse to compromise or we don't have the maturity to simply agree to disagree.

We are seeing so much of this behavior all over our culture these days, especially when it comes to politics or religion. While we know there is nothing new under the sun regarding conflict, we should learn from those that did it *incorrectly* and the ones who handled it *wisely*.

I have had conflict in every aspect of my life, and most times the conflict is due to giving into a knee-jerk reaction instead of choosing an attitude of peace. Proverbs 15:1 says, "A gentle answer turns away anger, but a harsh word stirs up wrath." If we would just obey this pattern of behavior, for the most part, we could avoid unnecessary and fruitless conflict.

So, what can we do in order to lessen conflict in our lives? My sweet friend Patsy Clairmont passed along some great advice to me many years ago. It has been a tremendous help to me, so I pass it down to you.

These exercises work in all sorts of relationships—whether that means marriage, friendships, family, or the workplace—in order to manage dysfunction and conflict. ◆

AS PATSY WOULD SAY:

DON'T CRITICIZE OR NITPICK.

In any relationship, make space for another person's humanity (man, that is so powerful!). When we apply this behavior, we have an understanding of God's deep graciousness.

DON'T POUT.

Pouting begins in the earliest stage of life; it is a learned behavior. First Corinthians 13:11 tells us to "put aside childish things." This includes pouting. It is manipulation.

KEEP CALM.

Tempers can be a tool of intimidation, and fear could be the very reason you get so upset. Don't use rage to put someone or something "under control." Put your efforts toward resolving instead of revenge.

TAKE RESPONSIBILITY FOR YOUR REACTIONS.

This means asking often: "Would you forgive me?" Forgiveness is not easy, but is necessary. We know forgiveness doesn't make the *other person* right, but it sets *us* free.

USE MANNERS.

In all relationships, take the opportunity to let people know that you appreciate them. "Please" and "thank you" are small words that do much good and bear much fruit.

What sorts of situations most often stir up conflict in your life? How do you usually respond?

What pieces of Scripture could you cling to in moments of conflict to help you gain better perspective and respond in a godly way?

Who in your life manages conflict very well? What about their example could you emulate?

What important lessons have you learned about conflict in your own life that you could pass down to others?

"A GENTLE ANSWER TURNS AWAY ANGER, BUT A HARSH WORD STIRS UP WRATH."

PROVERBS 15:1 CSB

PERSEVERANCE

Perseverance is something I have always marveled in others. Most people that I would consider heroes all have that same characteristic in them. They keep going through all types of obstacles, and somehow they endure. When most of us would have quit a long time ago, I find myself wondering what is it in these heroes that drives them to keep going?

One of these heroes for me is a young woman who I have seen walk through one of the darkest journeys imaginable. Her story is filled with abuse—both against her and her four children as well. She hit roadblock after roadblock in trying to save herself and her children. I honestly don't know how she is still standing under the weight of it all. So I asked her to share her secret of how she continued to persevere.

Here is what she said to me . . .

"In the darkest moments, God is in your midst. Though you feel forsaken, He is working. Some days it takes every bit of effort you can muster, but finding His grace and mercy and provision in your everyday is a huge part of what has gotten me through and continues to get me through. I believe in the power of gratitude and the importance of intentionally searching for it even when I feel empty. The more I practice thanking God out loud for the blessings in my life, the more I become aware of all the ways that He has held me and my children."

"When we slip down the muddy path of getting stuck in all the 'why' and 'how could you' questions, we question God's sovereignty and man's free will. This is a dead-end trail that will only blanket us in our despair. And I have, and do, spend my fair share of moments under this heavy burden. Until He reminds me of His unfathomable love! And as I search for glimpses of it, I am reminded of so many blessings, and the darkness lifts. It is a daily, often moment-by-moment exercise that takes practice and effort, so that it can reside in the forefront of my spirit, breaking through the worries, fears, and frustrations, and dissolving hopelessness. We cannot be hopeless if we are thankful."

Gratitude . . . I don't think I expected this to be her answer, but it sure did jolt me into reality. We all have something to be thankful for. It's in gratitude that we can get up and face a new day. One thing that we can *always* be thankful for is that Jesus loves us, died for us, and is there to see us through the best and worst of times. For my friend, that's enough. And the truth is, it's enough for all of us. ◆

Wisdom passed down from my oldest sister on how she practically pursues gratitude:

"I look for God's hand in the little things every day. Like the kind word of a coworker or friend. Also a smile and cheerful greeting from a perfect stranger. I've noticed that God often molds my schedule to be just what He has planned for my day. Relax in each moment. Read the Psalms aloud and let them help you direct the praise back to Him."

DONITA COOPER
my oldest sister

What have you learned about thankfulness in the midst of darkness? What story could you share to help others face a dark time with gratitude?

"WE CANNOT
BE HOPELESS
IF WE ARE
THANKFUL."

GRATITUDE

You've probably heard it said that people can be categorized into two types—"glass half full" people or "glass half empty" people. Generally speaking, these are two very opposing outlooks on life—but I don't think you are always simply one or the other. Certainly, some people are either more defeatist or hopeful by nature, but I have found that in following Christ there is a certain progression that takes place over time, and that is the moving of the heart from *entitlement* (focusing on the good things in life I think I deserve) to *gratitude* (focusing on the good things in life that I did nothing to deserve).

It's very easy for the "control freak" part of me to want things to go a certain way, and when that way is not met, my attitude is decidedly "glass half empty." Grumbling, complaining, nothing ever works out, Murphy's Law . . . you get it. However, as we grow in our faith and we look at life with a more "zoomed out" perspective, we see that our thankful posture toward God and life has nothing to do with our circumstances, and everything to do with Christ. It has nothing to do with where we are, and everything to do with where we are ultimately going. No matter what is going on in life, no matter how hard or challenging or dark, it doesn't take away the fact that Christ died for us. He secured our future with Him forever, and none of our hardships are going to last long in the big picture. Once we grasp this, true gratitude isn't far behind.

There is really a lot of freedom when you have the ability to enjoy whatever God's good gifts and simple pleasures are to you in this life, with no assumptions or notions that you deserve or will ever get more. Why would you need more, when you have Christ, who is everything we could ever want, who as Hebrews 12 puts it, gives us a coming kingdom that cannot be shaken? I have found when I rely on this kind of thinking, my glass is always half full. I am grateful to be alive, I can enjoy the good days, and I can persevere through the bad ones—all because of Christ.

In His mercy and goodness, God gives us all things—the sunny days, the power to get through the rainy days, and the endless days in eternity ahead of us all, where we will be with Him forever! How can our response be anything other than grateful? ◆

SHELLEY'S PRACTICAL TIPS TO
CULTIVATE GRATITUDE

When you find yourself dwelling on anything that you feel you lack or deserve but don't have, take a few minutes to counteract those thoughts by making a physical list of things that you *do* have that bring a sense of joy or fullness to your life.

Another thing that is helpful for me, and also brings joy to someone else, is saying "thank you" to at least one person you are grateful for every single day. Tell them, text them, email them—and let them know of your gratitude toward them.

What lessons has God taught you about gratitude that you could pass on to others?

"THEREFORE, SINCE WE ARE

RECEIVING  A KINGDOM

THAT CANNOT BE SHAKEN,

LET US BE **THANKFUL**."

HEBREWS 12:28 CSB

FEAR

My life verse—passed down to me from my mother when I was seventeen years old—is 2 Timothy 1:7, which says, "For God has not given us a spirit of fear, but one of power, love, and sound judgment." There's good reason behind this being my life verse, for it often helps me fight my biggest enemy: fear. Fear can cause a paralyzing effect within the mind that stifles the heart's ability to hope. I know it very well.

It was in October 1998 that our family received some news that would change our lives. My dad was diagnosed with leukemia. Before the news got to us, I was traveling nonstop at the time for work, but once it came, I found replacements for my upcoming commitments and booked it home to South Carolina. When I finally got to the hospital, my dad was in a state of extreme weakness, and I held him so tight. I asked the doctor, "If this were *your* dad, what would you do?" He said, "I would have him at the MD Anderson Cancer Center within twenty-four hours."

Fear set in like I've never experienced it before. I was so afraid of the unknown, but I was more afraid about the fear I saw overtaking my dad. I can vividly remember crying out to the Lord, begging Him to lift the fear from my sweet father. "Lord, allow me to carry some of this burden. He is so afraid. We all are . . . *please, Lord!* Help us in this fear."

I'm sure you have your own story of fear, or perhaps even cancer, in your own family. I don't know how it played out for you, but for me, I watched God do miracles, both in my dad's cancer case and in my own heart. We were able to get to that

center within twenty-four hours. We were treated kindly. Once examined, somehow the doctors said the cancer was not as bad as they originally thought. Funds for the treatment trickled in from family and friends. My entire family sacrificed whatever was going on in their schedules to rally around Dad when he needed it most. The Lord got my father through the terrible fear of the port being put in. God got me through many bouts of terror with moments of divine peace and nearness. The chemo worked. Total strangers became dear friends. I could mention a thousand more ways God moved for our family, but the most unbelievable part is that my dad is now cancer-free, for more than twenty years and counting!

Looking back on that season, I am so grateful to remember how truly personal God can be during times of fear. He was such a quiet assurance for us. Whether the outcome was good or bad—after all, not all news of cancer ends up with a story of remission—I knew God was *with* us, and that's what gets you through *any* sort of news. Even if my dad didn't end up cancer-free, God would have still been with us every step of the journey, and His presence is the thing that lifts all that fear, and brings you back to your senses. When God is in the equation, paralysis is not a given; power, love, and a sound mind really are possible with the Lord! ◆

What situation is most fearful for you right now? Why?

What passage of Scripture could help you experience God's nearness during this season of fear?

What evidences of God's help and nearness do you see in this season?

What has God taught you about fear in your own life? What wisdom would you pass down to others as they battle with fear?

"FOR GOD HAS NOT GIVEN US A SPIRIT OF FEAR,

BUT ONE OF POWER, LOVE AND SOUND JUDGMENT."

2 TIMOTHY 1:7 CSB

EXPECTATIONS

I hit my forties in stride. Whether it was being a career woman, a room mom at school, a booster club member, a Bible study leader—it seemed like I could be everything. Until things started falling apart.

I had started forgetting stuff, my eyesight had started to go, and other things had begun to sag. I was crying for no reason. I had a nagging ache that things weren't okay. Can you relate?

I found myself sitting on the couch of a counselor's office with tears streaming down my face wondering, *What is wrong with me?* I'm not miserable, I love my family, I love my church, I love my job, I love to laugh and sing.

The counselor began: "If I were to ask you to sing a song for me, could you do it?" I told him, "Yes, of course." It's what I do for a living, after all. Then he asked, "If I were to lay a bunch of bricks on you would you be able to sing?" I laughed, "Well, it would be pretty tough. I might be able to squeak out some notes." Then he asked the clincher: "What is weighing you down so much in life that it is making it hard for you to sing?"

I know it's not just one thing. I'm a people-pleaser. I want people around me to be happy. I feel responsible when they're not. Then there is the whole comparison problem and the expectations I have put on myself. Not just my physical appearance or abilities, but "Christian" things too. *Am I doing enough for others? Is God calling us to adopt? If not, what will people think? Have I taught my kids enough Scripture? Will they make bad choices because I'm not a good enough mom?*

I thought that as a "woman of faith" I would have it together by now, but I don't, and it took some time on that couch to remember the first song I ever learned. I bet you remember it too.

Jesus loves me, this I know,
for the Bible tells me so.

Somehow in the busyness of life, I had forgotten what I've known since I was a child. *Jesus loves me, period.* Not for how well I have it all together or how much I serve or what I look like in front of other people. It has been the most freeing realization, empowering me with grace to give others and myself instead of guilt.

Maybe, for you, it's not a bunch of tiresome little things. Maybe it's a big thing like cancer, unemployment, loss, betrayal, or a dysfunctional family. Whatever it is for you, may you not forget the song that rang true in my heart all those years ago. *Jesus loves me and He loves you, period.* I pray that you will allow this song to ring true to your own soul and that you will receive and open up His gift of grace and begin to sing your own song. ◆

"There are two ways to release expectations. The first is through intentional reflection, prayer, and feedback from a trusted friend, pastor, or counselor. Through that process, you can become aware and develop a new way of moving forward without these burdensome expectations. The second way is to wait until the weight of expectations become so unmanageable in your life that your world is crushed through poor choices, exhaustion, or broken relationships. I think it's an easy choice, but it's all your choice to make."

JEFF HELTON
my personal counselor, former pastor, coach, and consultant at WellSpring Coaching

Release the ideas in your mind of how you *think* things are supposed to be or how they are supposed to turn out. Let yourself "off the hook," giving yourself some grace and offering it to others as well.

Take time to access the things that you feel like the Lord has gifted you with. Doing this helps me be okay with saying "no" to certain things that I typically would guilt myself into doing because I feel like I would disappoint someone.

Sit and read Psalm 139 out loud. I do this sometimes to remind myself who I am and who created me. I'm not always going to please others. When I feel that tension, I have to ask myself, who is putting the expectation on me? Ultimately who am I created to please?

Read the lyrics or listen to the song "How He Loves." It's a powerful lyric and when I feel like I'm not measuring up, it's a good reminder of how God feels about me.

"Jesus loves me this I know."

What have you learned about releasing expectations? As you look back over all God has taught you, what one piece of wisdom would you share with others as they strive to release their own expectations in their relationships?

I'm not sure how I ended up with the topic of aging, as I am the youngest member of Point of Grace. It seems like it should have gone to Denise who is a whole forty days older than me, or at the very least, Leigh, who is thirteen days my senior. I feel certain they would have much more to offer on the subject—as they are so much more seasoned in life than me—but I'll do my best.

By the time this book releases, I will have just turned fifty years old. All of the things I used to hear people joking about, and found ridiculous, are coming true—"the wheels falling off," so to speak. I can read nothing without my glasses, my feet ache from fasciitis for a solid thirty minutes upon waking, and 24/7 hot flashes are my new reality.

AGING

Aging just is what it is. You never think it's going to happen to you, but if you are lucky enough to make it to fifty, let me assure you, it does.

For all the challenges of aging, I am grateful for one thing: with age comes wisdom and perspective. As believers we should be the most joyful "old people" around! Though the world might say we are getting the bad end of the deal, the truth is, we are just *exchanging* one good thing for another. We are just "trading in" our physical well-being for our mental and spiritual well-being—that's one way I like to look at the process of aging. Or, as 2 Corinthians 4:16 puts it, "Even though our outer person is being destroyed, our inner person is being renewed day by day."

Our bodies have indisputably passed their physical prime, but as believers, our minds are being renewed and regenerated. As Hebrews 12 famously tells us, if we are seeking to lock our eyes on Jesus each day, letting go of the things that don't matter and holding tight to the things that do, I'd say we have found the "secret sauce." The more we do this, the more our perspective changes, and the more we see this life for what it truly is—our temporary home where things might make us happy for a moment, but nothing truly satisfies the deep hunger in our heart for God. That is, except for more of God Himself. But to get more and more of God, you need more and more time with Him. Which is why aging is such a gift—it gives you that time to become transformed as the days go by.

So do not despise aging. I consider it a gift I get to unwrap a little more every day—in order to gain more understanding of where I'm going, and Who I'm going home *to*. ◆

"I'm old . . . still working on wise. Titus 2 tells us that older women should teach younger women. Such a blessing as a younger woman. Scary as an older woman! The wisest thing I've ever done is surround myself with wise people. Actually, God has put them everywhere I turn. The young are craving wise guidance. So, look to older, experienced, seasoned mentors whose path leads you home to Jesus."

BETH D. MOORE
my "older" neighbor and friend

What is your greatest fear about aging? Why?

What do you know about God now that you couldn't have known in your younger years? How does this encourage you about the process of aging?

What passage of Scripture has been most impactful to you as you've gotten older?

"EVEN THOUGH OUR OUTER

PERSON IS BEING DESTROYED,

OUR INNER PERSON

IS BEING RENEWED

DAY BY DAY."

2 CORINTHIANS 4:16 CSB

NEW JOB

No matter how a job comes your way, whether it's through a personal connection you have, applying online to endless employers and waiting for a response, or someone asking you to take a position you weren't expecting, trusting God with a new job can be hard.

I have gone through the "new job" phase four times in the last twenty-eight years. Everyone's experiences are different in this, but for me, three out of the four were "replacement" positions.

Anytime you are preceded by someone that was respected and extremely gifted in his or her position, it makes things very difficult in terms of self-confidence and comparison, doesn't it? So when I accepted the position of joining the Point of Grace family in October 2003, I was challenged to overcome those particular fears and insecurities head-on! Because Point of Grace had a tremendous reputation of excellence prior to me, I couldn't help but question my true ability to do the job and do it *well*!

I worked so hard to convince others that I was the right choice, that they should like me, that I was worthy of the opportunity. Many times, this made my job even more difficult and less enjoyable. I was so afraid to trust God in the talent He gave me and its contribution to the group that I ended up overcompensating—I started to become more of an actress than a true worshiper of the Lord in our songs and performances.

However, over this last decade, I've learned to be genuine with what God has given me. I have the talent I have, and it is enough for the goals of our group. I just need to trust Him with it and prepare well in my private time for my public contribution. The same is true for you. God's given you skills that He wants you to use, and you don't have to pretend to be better than you are. All you have to do is worship Him by using your gifts for His glory in whatever job He has for you, and develop those skills well as you go. He was faithful to bring you to this job, and He will be faithful to you in it! ◆

What has God taught you about a new job or the workplace in general? What advice could you pass on to someone else from your own experience?

LEIGH'S TIPS ON

MAKING THE MOST OF A NEW JOB

HERE ARE A FEW TIPS TO KEEP IN MIND AS YOU BEGIN A NEW JOB.
THEY CAN APPLY WHEREVER YOU ARE, IN WHATEVER YOU'RE DOING—WHETHER
A WAITRESS, STOCK BROKER, OR A BRAIN SURGEON!

BE PUNCTUAL. It's that simple. Being on time—or even a little bit early—communicates that you respect the position you hold and the time of others. Lack of punctuality communicates that you do not respect the position you've been given and that you don't value the time of those who are coming to meet you.

BE PREPARED. Know what is required of you and do it with excellence. This communicates that you appreciate your position and that you are not the sort of worker who would waste the time of others with an incomplete or haphazard presentation of yourself.

HAVE INTEGRITY. Let integrity be your mission. Integrity will cover all manner of work ethic and motivate your peers to pursue a higher standard in their work as well. This means no cutting corners, no cheating, no lying, no slandering, and no

straying from the sort of personal character Scripture outlines for all believers. To put it positively, it means doing a job thoroughly, doing it honestly, telling the truth, building others up, and staying consistent with the sort of Christian you say you are.

PERSEVERE. Not every job is a forever job. It's okay if this particular job isn't the one you want for the rest of your career. Some jobs are given to us by God for a season to develop our character, connect us to people who may have a role in our future, or minister to someone in that workplace. If you are in a season where you don't like your job, keep going. Invite the Lord into your frustration, and ask Him to soften your heart to those He may be trying to reach through you. When the time is right to move on, He will make it clear. In the meantime, stay faithful to Him and to the job required of you. After all, all of our work is done unto Him, no matter what it is or how long it lasts!

"USE YOUR GIFTS FOR GOD'S GLORY IN WHATEVER JOB HE HAS
FOR YOU, AND DEVELOP THE SKILLS HE'S GIVEN YOU AS YOU GO."

FRIENDSHIP

Friendships can come and go throughout seasons of life, but faith-based, Jesus-believing friendships last forever.

I have been blessed to have some of the sweetest of friendships. Walking life with someone requires trust in them, love for them knowing their worst and best qualities, and willingness to keep walking.

I have a dear friend named Kelley. We have walked a lot of miles together, both figuratively and literally. We met when Spence, my oldest son, was in kindergarten with her son Will.

We walk four or five times a week. I like to call it our free therapy. She knows my strengths and my weaknesses. She encourages me when I feel pretty low, and I encourage her when she is having a rough time too. When we are *both* down, well, let's just say it's a *long* walk. We have prayed about all kinds of things with kids, marriage, and families. However, my favorite thing about our friendship is that we have learned together to trust God with our stuff. Everyone needs a "Kelley" who can point them back to the Lord for all things. We can praise Him together, and we can cry to Him together.

One of my favorite Bible study leaders encourages women to find a friend who will tell you when something doesn't look good on you. And, though I'm sure you can already tell, she isn't just talking about clothes. She's talking about sinful characteristics that can get the better of all of us, whether that be jealousy or pride or many

other things. We all need someone who can see in us something better to put on, like forgiveness or kindness. The Bible calls this *speaking the truth in love*, and it's something good friends should do often.

Kelley isn't afraid to tell me that I need to give my husband a break or stop obsessing over something that is tempting me to have a bad attitude. If we don't have someone who can tell us the truth, we can start walking down a really tough road on our own. It's in those places we are isolated that the enemy loves to mess with our minds and wreak some havoc. But when we are with a friend, we can remind each other of what's true.

Ralph Waldo Emerson has been credited with the famous phrase: "The only way to have a friend is to be one." Are you willing to walk with someone on the hills, straightaways, and not so easy paths? If so, find that person. I promise it makes the journey much sweeter. ◆

I learned most of my friendship skills by observing my mom over the course of my life. Here are a few things I've learned from her example:

"First and foremost the easiest way to make friends is to be involved in things that you love. More than likely, those people are going to have some common interest. Our friends were from church, choir, sports, and school. Church friends were definitely a place where Christ is the commonality even if other interests aren't the same. Sunday school and Bible study will always be special places to connect with other women."

"Have people over to the house or meet for lunch. Ask them questions about themselves, and try not to talk so much about yourself."

"Just being kind and having a smile can go a long way. Genuinely care about others. I've watched my mom do this her entire life. People know a fake smile from something real."

JANICE MASTERS
my mom

What have you learned over the years about friends?

How has God developed you as a friend?

"THE ONLY WAY TO HAVE A FRIEND IS TO BE ONE."

—RALPH WALDO EMERSON

EXPECTING A BABY

It seems like yesterday that my husband Stu and I sat on a dock in Destin, Florida, discussing if it was time to consider starting our family. We'd been married for five years, Point of Grace was in full swing, and he was beginning to settle in as a Physician Assistant in the ER.

We definitely felt like it was time, but I was very apprehensive about how it was going to affect my life. I would be the first girl in Point of Grace to have a child. How were they going to feel about me bringing along a child while we were on the road? How would they feel if we would have to take some time off? This decision did not only affect Stu and me, but my fellow musicians too.

Having a baby can feel like it's going to change everything about your life. And, I suppose it does in many ways. Your social life changes, you have to be more on a schedule, finances can be a little more challenging. Every day will cause you to learn more about yourself and all the things you don't know. You will make all kinds of mistakes, and you will clean up all sorts of messes. There will be proud moments and humiliating moments, highs and lows. You will love being called "mommy" one day, and then the next day you may wish you could change your name because you hear it over and over again. Sounding fun yet?

Here's something wonderful about becoming a parent that I didn't expect: you will know about love in a way that you've never experienced before. Your perspective on God's love for you will be changed as well. My best advice about the journey

is to take each stage and say to yourself: *This is the best season.* Gratitude will help ground you when things seem out of control.

Parenthood is a journey like no other, and your life will be richer and fuller for having experienced it. It will bring you to a dependency on God that will change you for the better. Pray, pray, pray for your children. And remember, you aren't raising them alone. God will bless you with friends, coaches, and teachers who will walk beside them as well. It takes a village. Enjoy the ride! ◆

"Enjoy and embrace each season in your child's life! 'Go through it' and 'grow through it' together with God as your guide. Giggle . . . belly laugh . . . cry . . . share emotions . . . and most important, pray God's Word over your children."

LORI BECKLER
*my mentor, friend, and founder of the
Heritage Keepers Conference*

What phase of parenthood are you most afraid of? Why?

*What woman in your life can you bring into these fears
and learn from?*

DENISE'S PRACTICAL TIPS
FOR EACH PHASE OF PARENTING

1 **INFANTS:** Nothing is sweeter than holding this little gift. Hold them any chance you get! And when you can't keep your eyes open, ask for help.

2 **TERRIBLE TWOS:** Calling it "Terrific Twos" in the moment can make the tantrums a bit more manageable, and even laughable at times.

3 **STARTING SCHOOL:** Enjoy watching them meet new friends (and don't forget to make some yourself!). Enjoy watching them develop.

4 **MIDDLE SCHOOL:** Have fun being their personal driver, and help them navigate through all the changes that middle school can bring (hormones, acne, rejection, the list goes on).

5 **HIGH SCHOOL:** Find ways to engage with them and be their biggest cheerleader no matter what the activity. They will remember that you cared about their interests and showed up when it mattered.

6 **COLLEGE:** Enjoy watching them develop into adulthood. But don't think your job is over just yet. They still need you!

"PARENTHOOD BRINGS YOU TO A DEPENDENCY ON GOD THAT WILL CHANGE YOU FOR THE BETTER."

MOTHERHOOD

Motherhood. Such a loaded word. There are so many emotions, duties, responsibilities, and expectations attached to it that once you become a mother, it seems impossible to wrap your head around it all. No amount of preparation, strategizing, or good old-fashioned control can ensure that you will have a happy and successful child. I realized this very early on in my motherhood journey, and it was sobering and scary—especially with the dawn of the information age where endless parenting books, conferences, and videos on "how to get it right" were constantly in my face.

For the first several years of my daughter Caroline's life, I was trying to do my best to decipher the correct technique for discipling, scheduling, choosing friends, choosing schools, and any and everything else that seemed important. It can get pretty overwhelming in this fast-paced culture we all find ourselves in, making you feel like you're on a hamster wheel, going nowhere fast and having no real focus in your parenting approach.

Fast-forward to Caroline's 4th grade year. I happened upon a small and unassuming Bible study made up of moms during that time, and to say I was blessed by this would be an understatement. A wise and godly pastor named Don led our group, and honestly, he rescued us from ourselves as we were trying to trudge through the book of Leviticus on our own!

That little study turned into five years of Bible instruction under Pastor Don. I learned more about God's Word in those five years than I have in all the rest combined! Don was indeed equal parts humility and wisdom. During one lesson, he said something that absolutely realigned my parenting goals and got me off the hamster wheel. I have never gotten back on. I remember that he looked at us moms, some of us barely hanging on trying to keep up with all that we had going on, and he said,

"You have *the* most important job in the world as a mother, and that is to pass along the story of Jesus. Make sure your children know it. It should be central. *Teach* them the story. Rely on no one else—not a teacher or a friend or a youth group leader."

I remember leaving that day and thinking to myself, *Shelley, if you don't do* anything *else well, get that right. If you get that right, nothing else really matters.*

It should have been so obvious—but do you know how freeing that was for me to hear? I stopped playing the comparison game, the perfection game, and I went into "just teach the story" mode from that point on. My only mission as a mom was to pass on the story of Jesus, and simply focusing on this affected pretty much everything else.

We have to remember that we are not responsible for what our kids *do* with what we teach them; that part they have to own themselves. We are simply responsible for doing the teaching part, helping them understand the story of Jesus, and hopefully, following Him because of it. My prayer has always been that on the day I say good-bye to Caroline at college, turn around and walk away, that I won't have missed it. Just teach the story of Jesus—that's the mark of true parenting success. ◆

"When I think about motherhood, I think about intentionality. I want to be intentional about talking about God, His Word, His story in the casual conversations we have every day . . . around the lunch table, in the car on the way to sporting events, sitting doing arts and crafts together, quiet times just before turning out the light at night. 'Teach them [God's words] to your children, talking about them when you sit in your house and when you walk along the road, when you lie down and when you get up' (Deut. 11:19). Be intentional to keep the main thing the main thing."

TERRI WOOD
my friend

What parenting lessons has God taught you over the years as a mother?

What bits of wisdom or advice would you pass on to other current or future mothers?

"Just teach the story of Jesus.

That's the mark of true parenting success."

PARENTING

A lot of people don't know that my husband and I had our first child after ten years of marriage. And in that particular season, we were in airports and on tour buses so much, we just assumed we were "one and done." Because I was the baby of two older sisters and loved growing up with siblings, I did struggle with our daughter being an only child. But I pressed out the "what-ifs" and pressed on in our current plan. *Until.*

When my daughter was nine years old, I joined a Bible study entitled *Jonah: Navigating a Life Interrupted* by Priscilla Shirer. I had no idea during that time of study, God was preparing my heart for an amazing, well, *interruption.* One that would come about nine months later.

We had just celebrated our 20th wedding anniversary when we found out we were pregnant with baby number two. This was just before my 43rd birthday. Yes. *43rd birthday.* In fact, when I called my parents to tell them the fantastic news my mom insisted that I stop joking around!

LATER IN LIFE

The usual fears around getting pregnant later in life immediately descended on myself, my husband, and yes, even my daughter (when she heard the news she'd have to share her things, she screamed in horror). We all just kept having to remind ourselves this was really happening. And then, on Thanksgiving Day 2012, we brought home our baby boy, and life has never been more precious or extremely loud! Andy keeps us moving and makes us appreciate the unexpected joys that can come later in life.

Parenting at this age has challenges, sure. I'm tired quicker, I can't sit criss-cross applesauce, and I have to tell people I am not his grand-mother. But the benefits outweigh all the frustration—you appreci-ate anew the miracle of birth, you're not in a rush for certain ages to hurry up, you seem to leave more time to reflect on all of life's simple achievements, and holidays give you the chance to see through the eyes of a little one again. It's amazing.

God interrupted my life and asked me to parent a little one far past the time I thought I ever would. And on the other side of the sur-prise, a blessing was waiting. If I could tell you anything, with parent-ing later in life or with anything, really, be willing to let God interrupt you, surprise you, and bless you. It's worth it. ◆

When I was pregnant with my daughter, I had the privilege to sit down with ten teenage girls and ask their advice (these girls were at the "House of Hope" home in Orlando, Florida) . . . here is what they advised.

"First, actually listen when we talk (stop what you're doing, and really look into our faces). Second, ask us the hard questions! And third, ask us the hard questions AGAIN. Why? Because the first time you asked, we were watching for your reaction, wondering, is it safe to be truthful?"

Have you or anyone you know been asked by God to parent later in life?

What was that like?

How did you lean on Him?

Who did He bring along to help you?

74

"BE WILLING TO LET GOD INTERRUPT YOU, SURPRISE YOU, AND BLESS YOU."

RAISING THE NEXT GENERATION

So far, I have sixteen years of parenting experience. While I've certainly learned a lot, I don't feel worthy by *any* stretch to be giving out advice on raising kids. However, I have given it a lot of thought when thinking about this particular essay. First and foremost, I have learned it's really good to have lots of grace and zero judgment when it comes to parents who don't do things like I do. We are all on our own journey—learning as we go. After a lot of pondering and praying, I have come up with three overriding thoughts that I'd love to pass on to you; things that I have tried my best to do thus far in my journey as a parent. Here goes . . .

1. CONSIDER AND STEWARD YOUR CHILD'S HEART ABOVE ALL ELSE—AND DON'T GET CAUGHT IN THE COMPARISON TRAP.

It is so tempting and easy from the day your child is born to compare their progress and accomplishments against another child's. When did she roll over? When did she start walking? Fast-forward a few years and it's "What is her GPA?" While all of these things matter on some level to parents, none of them have a thing to do with what is most important—and that is your child's heart.

I once heard something in a sermon that I'll never forget: "There is no 'win' in comparison. It is of no help to look right or to look left. Only keep your eyes fixed straight ahead." We love this sort of advice for ourselves in our struggle with comparison, but we forget it also applies to the way we view and raise our children. They are unique and individual, and we have to remember that not a single earthly accomplishment will have any eternal value, except for where their heart's allegiance ultimately lies. Steward their heart and character before anything else, and enjoy their milestones as God brings them.

2. YOUR EXAMPLE—THE MINUTE-BY-MINUTE AND DAY-BY-DAY MODEL YOU SET—IS ULTIMATELY WHAT THEY WILL BECOME.

Very sobering I know, but accurate. The apple truly doesn't fall far from the tree. Your child will pick up the best and worst of your traits. I know that's the truth in my household. It's just the way it is. There are millions of parenting books—you could never read them all. It's overwhelming. Instead of looking to those books, look to *the* book to help you learn what you should be modeling to your child. Talk about God in your homes, read His Word together as a family, model Christ in the best way you know how, and when you fail, simply admit it, repent and apologize, and then move on. This is called *sanctification*, and your child needs to see it happening in you until the day you die—this is where they will truly learn that God *can* and *does* change a person, little by little.

3. PASS DOWN THE STORY OF JESUS.

I've already mentioned this once in another essay, but I'll reinforce it here because of its importance. It is *so* imperative that our kids have a genuine understanding of the gospel *before* they leave our nests, whether they believe it for themselves at this stage or not. Similarly, we can't rely on church, a Christian school, a pastor, or any other means to impart to our kids a genuine understanding of the Scriptures. If we miss this, our kids lose. They will miss out on understanding who God really is, and when they leave us, the world will fill in the gaps for them.

A family that I really admire had this quote by Theodore Roosevelt written on the chalkboard in their kitchen while their four daughters were growing up. It said, "A thorough knowledge of the Bible is worth more than a college education." This is something that we should keep in the forefront of our minds as we raise the next generation. ◆

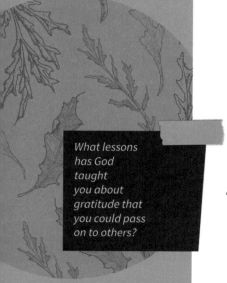

What lessons has God taught you about gratitude that you could pass on to others?

TEACHING YOUR KIDS ABOUT JESUS AND SCRIPTURE

Reading to your kids before bed is always a sweet time to allow them to wind down and truly focus on what you are saying. It's really the only time you have a somewhat quiet and captive audience when they are young. I always tried not to waste this sort of "set in stone every night" time on "cute" books alone. I made an intentional effort to read at least part of a chapter from a children's story Bible in addition to the required *Curious George* or whatever the flavor of the day was.

We also had a little drawer in our kitchen table where we kept a devotional book or Bible when Caroline was past the "reading before bed" age. Every night after dinner, David or I would pull out that book, which was very conveniently located, and either read a devotional or a small bit of a Bible chapter and discuss it before we would start the dishes.

Look for built-in times that are occurring anyway—e.g., dinner, bedtime, car ride to school, etc., and use those times to talk about God.

> "A thorough knowledge of the Bible is worth more than a college education."
>
> —Theodore Roosevelt

FAMILY
FUN

Finding opportunities to have fun has never been difficult for my family. We are all about interaction, mystery, and adventure. We have found this allows our family to unplug from technology and make unforgettable memories.

You might wonder where our tradition of adventure came from. Enter my Aunt Wren. Of everyone in my family, Aunt Wren is the master of creativity. She is so extraordinary, in fact, that her ideas have influenced our family activities for more than twenty-five years now.

It all started when my extended family went to a Mystery Theme Dinner in Atlanta, Georgia. At that time, it was a party of ten. Now we are a party of seventeen and counting. This dinner showed us the fulfillment of being together, laughing, and realizing how much we enjoy each other's company.

What are some fun family traditions you could record here to pass on to others?

Since then, Aunt Wren has helped organize murder mysteries, scavenger hunts, vacation adventures, painting parties, and the list goes on and on. The woman makes Pinterest look like child's play. She has set such a precedent in her intentionality for fun, and the kids love to anticipate what she will do next for the holidays, vacations, and special events. Aunt Wren has helped all of us want to explore our creative side as well.

One of our favorite adventures she organized was a game of "Survivor" while on family vacation. Each evening we had tribal competitions, such as blind tastings and filling a bucket with ocean water using only a sponge, concluding with tribal counsel. Aunt Wren's thoughtful planning made our vacation extra special, and everyone in the family still talks about that week!

The years are filled with Aunt Wren's shenanigans, and we are all better for it. She has truly taught us that the abundant life God offers includes flat-out fun.

So whoever you are, wherever you are, and whatever the adventure looks like, jump in. Plan it. Bring the whole family along, and make a memory that will shape the life of your family forever. Be Aunt Wren to someone. They'll thank you for it. ◆

"The abundant life God offers includes

FOR HAVING FAMILY FUN

DO A HOLIDAY SCAVENGER HUNT. Each team documents the hunted item by taking a picture of the team with the item. At the end of the hunt, use the pictures to create a memorable Christmas album full of family fun in each shot.

GAME NIGHT. These can be puzzles, buzzer games, card games, board games, or mystery games. Choose whatever your family loves, and as a bonus, turn technology off. You'll see how quickly your time together turns into laughter and connection!

PICKLE BALL. Aunt Wren introduced us to this, and now she gets to introduce you to it! It is perfect for any age group—young and old. This allows your family to get in some much-needed exercise while on vacation or during the holidays. The instructions are easily found online, and let me tell you, it is a hoot!

RUN OR WALK A 5K ON THANKSGIVING. This would work for any other holiday as well, and gets your family active, usually for a good cause! Thanks to my Aunt Lark's inspiration, our family participates in the 5K Turkey Trot every year.

flat-out fun."

CHANGE

As I write this, my youngest son, Price, will be graduating from high school in six weeks. The sadness has begun to creep into my heart. Make no mistake, I am excited for him and his future, but there is a grieving process that happens when they take that step across the stage to get that diploma. At least I know what to expect this time around.

However, it's hard to forecast when the tears will come, and usually they rain down when you least expect it. The fears of the "what-ifs" tend to overtake my mind. *What if he's not ready? What if he doesn't make new friends or makes too many new friends? What if he flunks out? What if he completely walks away from God?*

Graduation means change, and if you're like me, I'm not crazy about change. All of us experience change. New job, new house, new city, new school, new diagnosis. I grieve the old and fear the new, and I don't accept it very well. But here's something I've learned that I'd love to pass on to you: it's how we deal with the middle section between the old and new that makes the difference.

I once heard a psychologist say we are not preparing the next generation to deal with change very well. When things don't go exactly as we expect, we become depressed and lose hope quickly. The truth is, it's okay to grieve and it's okay not to know *what* the future looks like. What we do have to know is *Who* holds our future and trust Him in the transition period.

Think about the Saturday between Good Friday and Easter. The week had been a roller coaster. First, Jesus parades into town on a donkey, people are waving palm branches and singing praises to God. His disciples are probably elated at the possibilities ahead.

But then things turn absolutely horrible. The unimaginable happens as Jesus is betrayed, arrested, beaten, and then hangs on the cross. Saturday comes and they are at a loss. Things definitely did not turn out the way they thought. I can just hear the silence as they sit, huddled together. Jesus told them what would happen, but at the time, I don't think they could really comprehend it. What amazes me is while they are sitting in the dark not knowing what to do,

Jesus was breaking down the walls of sin and death on our behalf so we could all experience full and complete redemption. Sunday was coming, and they had no idea.

When we hit those moments in life that feel like the Saturday in-between—which for me right now is graduation for my son—we can't forget that God has plans for our lives and for the lives of our kids. Plans to eventually prosper and not harm us, to give us hope and a future, whether in this life or the one to come (Jer. 29:11). God is at work in the middle of our funk. He knows what's coming, and He's got us—and all of it really—in the palm of His hand. No matter what we face, highs or lows, cheering voices or silent huddled sorrow, kids leaving our nest and stepping out into the world, I've learned a valuable lesson that can get us through it all: Sunday is coming! God will see them through to the other side, and us too.

This piece of wisdom, in the form of an acrostic, is from my former Ouachitones director at Ouachita Baptist University.

"TAGALS" stands for:

T—Trust

A—Adjust

G—Good

A—Attitude

L—Love

S—Sparkle

When I face new things or hard things, I often remember this phrase, and it helps me to trust God and be flexible. Bringing TAGALS to mind helps me choose a positive attitude, believing that God has it under control. So thankful for Mrs. Mary Shambarger's beautiful example, as it has allowed me to walk with love and joy at whatever change is in front of me. ◆

"Because God is good and omniscient, I've learned I don't have to know the whole plan. I can just trust Him with the next step right in front of me."

DAYNA COOPER
my middle sister

What scares you most about the changes transpiring in your life right now?

What fears overtake you sometimes?

What truths can you claim to overcome these fears?

What have you learned about transitions and changes in life?

How have you coped?

"GOD KNOWS WHAT'S

COMING, AND HE'S

GOT IT ALL IN THE

PALM OF HIS HAND."

WORRY

For as long as I can remember, I've been a worrier. I am a professional. I will worry about the future, what's in the news, my child—you name it. I will also take on *your* worry so you don't have to! Isn't that kind of me! In particular, I'm always worried that *something* is wrong with my health. For example, if I find a suspicious spot on my skin, I instantly think—melanoma!

I've always envied those who don't have the tendency to immediately go to the worst-case scenario in their minds. My husband is one of those people. When I'm going to the bad place, he will often say, "Babe, how many of your worries have even ended up coming true?" Naturally, I want to yell, "STOP BEING SO SENSIBLE!" But when you are in the pit of worry, rational thought just doesn't happen.

Denise is also one of those people. Any time I share with her one of my ridiculous worst-case scenarios, she says, "I would never even *think* to go there in my head!" I'm always envious of her outlook and think to myself, *Wow, how logical and freeing to live like that!*

God gave us a mind to reason, and His Word shows us that all worry is rooted in fear and the illusion of control. He doesn't want us to spend our days enslaved in anxiety. Yet, there have been many seasons when I have been. So, what to do? I know it's different for everyone, but something that has worked for me is to simply practice *remembering*.

Remembering that God is *for* me—and even if my worst fears are realized, I will ultimately be not just okay, but in the very palm of God's hand during the difficulties.

Remembering His Word—especially John 14:1, where Jesus tells me, "Don't let your heart be troubled. Believe in God; believe also in me." He is the ultimate ruler and timekeeper of every minute we have, and believing in how big He is pushes out all that worry!

Remember that the enemy wants to steal our days but that *we don't have to let him* take another from us!

A few years ago on vacation, my friend Jeff and I were sitting on the beach lamenting about our shared tendency to excessively worry. We were discussing John 10:10, "A thief comes only to steal and kill and destroy . . ." Jeff made the point that our life is like a book—we only have a certain number of pages, or days. It has been predetermined. Every day that we fill with worry instead of living in freedom is like the enemy ripping a page out of our book and discarding it.

I have never forgotten that mental picture. Sadly, *chapters* of my book are gone. So now, when I start down the rabbit hole of worry, I ask God to give me the strength I need to say "no." I am determined to not let Satan steal another one of my pages. While I can't change the past, I certainly have the power of the Holy Spirit to make sure the rest of my pages stay intact. Every day is a gift. Don't throw one away on worry. Believe God. He is for you, He is able, and He's got this, whatever it is. ◆

"I know exactly where Shelley gets her worrying from—that would be me! It's certainly not her dad. He's always said he doesn't need to worry about anything because I do enough for both of us! God's Word tells us in so many different verses not to worry. The thing that helps me most is to keep in close communication with God. Release your worries into God's care and pray about it often! Instead of worrying, we should focus on the promises of God's Word that give us hope, even in difficult situations."

SHARON PHILLIPS
my mom

What has God taught you about worry in your own life?

What pieces of wisdom would you pass down to a friend or family member about your experience in this?

"DON'T LET YOUR HEART BE TROUBLED. BELIEVE IN GOD; BELIEVE ALSO IN ME."

JOHN 14:1 CSB

COLLEGE

Going to college is such a privilege, isn't it? It is a place to delve into a deeper education and hopefully enhance your career opportunities. It's also a place to expand your comprehension of the needs and cultural differences of others in this world. It introduces you to lifelong relationships where you can see the value of others who are unlike you in the best of ways—which may result in an understanding and compassion you never had before. This phase in life forces us to step out of our "safe environment" and move into the season of adulthood.

Ecclesiastes 3 tells us there's a time to gather, and a time to scatter, a time to hold close, and a time to let go. College is the time we scatter from the home we were once gathered in, a time we let go from what we once knew as we come into our own.

My college experience started out like most. I was intimidated the first few semesters, but gradually became more and more comfortable. Sometimes that comfort was a good thing—a time for me to grow more confident in my own skin. Other times that comfort was a bad thing in that it loosened my ropes of conviction. That being said, as I look back, I like to tell others that college should be a time to flourish in such a way to build your faith and your career with confidence and a community of fellowship. (College sporting events can make that community of fellowship so much fun too!)

At the end of the day, if I could do it *all* over again, I would:

If you are the one heading to college, what fears do you have about starting this new educational journey?

What commitments can you make today that will help you get the most out of your college experience?

How will you incorporate your faith in this part of your story?

If you are a parent of a college-aged child, what fears do you battle as they go off to school?

What promises of God can you cling to as you face this new season?

Take some time to record the biggest lessons learned during your own college experience.

Spend more time working on those areas where I needed improvement instead of relying on what was natural and easy. For me, singing came naturally, but playing the piano and reading music was quite the challenge. For you, it might look different. Take the time to build into the weaker areas of your character and skills.

Respect my parents' investment and the resources that were at my disposal—I see now just how numerous they were! For example, most professors *love* helping students that want to learn! I regret not asking for their help and expertise. I can't go back and invite their wisdom and help now, and I wish I would have.

Find a spiritual community and mentor. College can be a place we drift from our faith. Instead of that, proactively planning to find a tight-knit faith community is essential. Try to find a local church or campus ministry where other solid believers are helping you along in this season of life. And don't underestimate the power of a spiritual mentor—a strong example of faith who can pour into you and build you up in the Lord!

Consider a less expensive educational option. College costs are rising, and there are options out there that do not require you to break the bank or exit college with an enormous amount of student loan debt. Some states even offer the first two years free; that's what we will encourage our own kids to do unless they get full scholarships elsewhere. No reason to have a mountain of debt to add to the other new challenges of adulthood once you graduate! ◆

"Every believer has been endowed with a spiritual gift (or gifts) to be used for His purpose. College is an opportunity to use your gift and build upon your God-given talents. Although you still have the support of family from a distance, college is your first step into managing life on your own. You have to take responsibility for getting to class on time, meeting assignment deadlines, taking care of personal needs, etc. Your choices reveal your character. May you always choose paths that reflect godly wisdom" Prov. 4:5–6.

ROBIN DARBY
my mother

"THERE'S A TIME TO GATHER, AND A TIME TO SCATTER, A TIME TO HOLD CLOSE, AND A TIME TO LET GO."

IDOLS

> **Most of us think of idols as a big golden cow or statue that we learned about in the Old Testament.**

If you're like me, sometimes I read those stories and think to myself, *Seriously? Who wants to worship a big cow?* After all, God had just performed some amazing miracles for the Israelites, such as parting the Red Sea, providing manna to eat, and water gushing from a rock in the desert! But I'm reminded of the line in the old hymn "Come Thou Fount" where it says, "Prone to wander, Lord, I feel it. Prone to leave the God I love . . ."

I grew up loving sports. To me, there's nothing like the excitement of a big game. And though many people don't know this, here's a fun fact: When Stu and I had children, we named our kids according to how it might sound over a loud speaker. As embarrassing as that sounds, it's true! So, given that Mom and Dad had a sports obsession, it was not hard for our kids to follow suit.

There is so much pressure these days on parents to make sure your child is in the right school, on the right team, has the right coach, and so on. For a while, I jumped on this train.

First of all, we had a child that excelled in athletics and dreamed of playing in college. We wanted to do the right thing to make sure he had all of the opportunities to help him achieve that goal. Second, he had the work ethic to want to get there. However, it became so stressful as I let it become the focus and center of everything we did. It was what I thought about constantly, worried about, and planned around. Sports had become *my* golden cow.

Through some injuries and other obstacles, God really got my attention. It put me on my knees. He showed me how out of whack my priorities were. Now, hear me say, it isn't wrong to put your children in sports or give them opportunities to excel with the gifts God has given them. But, it is wrong to worship these things. For me, I knew I had to turn it over to God, *daily* (sometimes even minute to minute!).

The first thing I have to do when realizing something has taken the place of the Lord is repent and just tell God how sorry I am. Sometimes, I'm required to take a break from certain activities that cause me to get out of whack.

Sometimes I've had to remove myself from people in my life that cause me to throw that idol back up on the shelf.

I also have had to get my calendar back out and take note of what I'm doing and how that could be affecting what takes over my mind and heart.

What I'm learning as I repent often is this: my child's story is in God's hands, and what He has written for them is much better and more than I could have ever imagined.

It may not be sports for you. It could be having the perfect house, the perfect family, the perfect job, the perfect body, a perfect romance, or a dozen other things. But friend, we must remember that God tells us to flee from idolatry. In fact, throughout Scripture He constantly warns us about how seriously He takes this offense! He knows we are prone to wander and desperately need His help to remind us of His greatness.

I love how Eugene Peterson paraphrases Psalm 86:8–10 in *The Message*:

> There's no one quite like you among the gods, O Lord, and nothing to compare with your works. All the nations you made are on their way, ready to give honor to you, O Lord, Ready to put your beauty on display, parading your greatness, And the great things you do—God, you're the one, there's no one but you!

Yours might not be the sports situation with your kid right now, but take some time to think about what your golden cow might be. I continue to pray and ask God to show me any other idols in my life. He's always faithful to show His truth, in love, and He is faithful to you too. ◆

What makes you most worried or keeps you up at night?

What do you find yourself thinking most about?

What, if taken away from you, would destroy you?

"GOD,

YOU'RE

THE ONE,

THERE'S NO ONE BUT

YOU!"

PSALM 86:10 MSG

WHITE SPACE

Church, husband, children, work, ministry, relationships, maintaining a home—it can all feel so overwhelming at times, and people often ask us how we balance it all. We usually laugh and give our three-word response—"Not very well!" It is definitely still a work in progress for all of us.

In a perfect world we could all work when the sun rises, and rest when it goes down. Yet, we find ourselves catching up on household tasks well into the evening, making lists for the next day, packing lunches, or returning phone calls and emails. Even when we should rest, we feel as if we can't. There is no margin or room for error in our lives. What's worse is that this level of busyness is often seen as a good thing in our culture, a badge of honor, even.

We could blame this on any number of things: our fast-paced technological age, higher demands on our children, the cost of living—you name it! But the truth is—*we* are the only ones who say *yes* and *no* to all the things that live on our calendar.

There's a wise and godly woman named Terri in my life who has successfully raised four daughters while maintaining a generally joyous home. While she would be the first to say she's not perfect, to me she's one of those people that exude a general peacefulness and grace no matter how busy she is. She is always willing to give me her time for a quick walk or talk, and on one of those walks years ago, she told me something that I still try to incorporate into my own life today. As I was complaining about how busy I was, she simply reminded me of the importance of *margin* in our schedules. I like to think of it as "white space" in the literal sense, where nothing is written in that day's space on my calendar. Time to be interrupted for a divine appointment. Time in our day for things to breathe and be flexible. Time for quiet.

To integrate Terri's advice for margin in my calendar, I do a few things. First, I write everything except birthdays down in pencil—because everything else has the potential to change. Next, when I'm not on the road, I try to leave white space on a day or two per week with nothing on them, days of margin. When I see that white space, I always get excited about what the Lord might have planned for me on those days. We could all easily fill our calendars with lots of good things every minute of every day, but it doesn't mean we should.

After some time of doing this, I've noticed God usually fills in that time with exactly what I need. If someone needs last-minute help—or to talk over a problem—I love being able to say "yes." Other times, the day remains free, and God steers me toward rest I didn't know I needed. Either way, penciling in margin gives me a tangible way to allow God to alter my week.

As you plan your days, don't miss what God might have for you by scheduling so tightly that your course can't be redirected. Give God your margin, your white space, and see what He does! ◆

What has God taught you over the years about the need for margin in your life?

How have you seen Him use your "white space" in unexpected ways?

What advice would you pass on to others about the value of margin?

Determine what things in your day are nonnegotiable and actually write them in your calendar as a gentle reminder when you are scheduling other appointments or activities. (Non-negotiables might include time with God, cooking for your family, etc.)

Keep a running list of errands that are NOT time sensitive. Knock them all out at once when your list gets five or ten things on it. In other words, one carefully plotted errand trip gives you more margin on your other days.

Don't feel like you have to say yes to everything or have a long drawn-out excuse when you do say no. I wish I were more like my husband who is very comfortable simply saying, "I wish I could, but I can't."

"Give God your margin, your white space, and see what He does!"

IN-LAWS

I've heard that the term *in-law* came about in the fourteenth or fifteenth century. The idea behind it is that your in-laws have the same rights, honors, and duties as your biological parents, which are transferred to them through the legal pact of marriage. For some families, this new reality may not be very welcome, but in other cases, it is very welcome indeed. For better or worse, the term is about parental responsibility over a new child in the family.

My husband and I have been married more than twenty-seven years, and it took time for me to appreciate that title as well as to respect the ones that held it. We live more than 900 miles away from my in-laws (our sure-fire way of keeping those relationships "healthy"), but my mother-in-law comes in town periodically to help with our kids when both of us have to travel.

Having an in-law fly in to help with the kids might sound picture-perfect to you. Yes, the good times have been really good, but the hard times have been hard too! I've faced seasons of jealousy toward my mother-in-law, whether that was due to some character trait she had that I wanted or the closeness she had with certain members of our family. But over the years, through time and through prayer, God has changed my way of thinking.

I now can see many ways God has taught me through her example. For instance, I've learned so much about my husband and his family's traditions, and my kids have been privileged to see firsthand the love she has for God and for them. I've also seen a deep mother-and-son relationship. Through the years, I've watched this beautiful lady serve us at various points with utter joy and gratitude.

So what was the difference-maker? How does one experience such a perspective shift? The prayer that changed things for me was: "God, help me see her the way You do." And you know what? He did! Her obvious differences from me no longer paralyzed me with frustration, but instead just made me laugh. I was free to be thankful for the ways she served our family instead of focusing on all the things she didn't do "right" in my mind. I could appreciate the ways God made her unique.

God helped me see these things, and He can help you too, if you struggle with your in-laws. They are gifts from Him, in all their shapes, sizes, and situations. All we have to do is ask for Him to help us see them through *His* eyes instead of our own. And the best part is, He will do this very same thing for our sons and daughters-in-law when they need help navigating a new life with *us* in their family! ◆

"IN-LAWS ARE GIFTS FROM GOD, IN ALL THEIR SHAPES, SIZES, AND SITUATIONS."

HOW TO APPRECIATE YOUR IN-LAWS

ASK GOD TO HELP YOU SEE THEIR GOOD QUALITIES, AND FOCUS ON THOSE.

DON'T JUDGE BEHAVIOR UNTIL YOU KNOW THEIR WHOLE HISTORY. For example, those that lived through the Depression hold a different value system than those that had everything handed to them. God can help you have an understanding, which results in a respect. Also, things they are adamantly against might stem from a family history of wounds when it comes to that particular area or habit going on in your own household.

REMEMBER THE "YOU SPOT IT, YOU GOT IT" PRINCIPLE. Things that usually bother you may be the very thing that is in you that bothers someone else. If you get annoyed at someone else's critical nature, for example, you can likely spot it quickly because *you* are that way! This principle breeds humility as you engage with your in-laws.

PUT PICTURES OF THEM IN YOUR HOME. That makes anyone feel loved and appreciated! And it also reminds you to pray for them, call them, and talk about them with your kids.

ADJUST THE TITLE YOU GIVE THEM. This will soften your heart toward them. One of my dear friends did this very thing—she purposefully called her in-laws "in-loves" so she could remember that their bond was one of love and not of duty.

MAKE A LIST OF THE WAYS *YOU* WOULD WANT TO BE TREATED. You will become a mother- or father-in-law as your own kids grow up and get married. Then ask yourself: *Am I treating my own in-laws this way?*

LAST, GET TO KNOW THEM! Do you know their middle name? Why they were named that? What about their dreams . . . did they become what they hoped? People don't mind telling you about themselves as long as it feels safe. It's probably been a while since anyone has asked them questions like these, so be a person who is genuinely interested in their stories, hearts, and lives.

What has God taught you about interacting with in-laws that you could pass on to someone else?

What advice would you offer?

THE POWER OF WORDS

One of my spiritual mentors, Shawna Keller, reminded me of something important in her Bible study on Proverbs—*My Mouth Matters*. Dana (our guitar player) is always chanting the phrase, "words that hurt, words that heal." Through these two people and countless others, I'm often reminded that we have power in our words. Sadly, there are some words I've said that have forever changed some relationships.

I have a dear and precious friend that comes to my mind. I said some things that I can never take back. God has forgiven me, and I have been forgiven by this friend, but still . . . The healing has happened, but the scars remain. Perhaps you have been through something similar, something you regret. For my friend and me, our relationship remains but still isn't quite the same. And what was lost between us is because of my own sin and words I said. Sin always results in death. Not just physical death, but death to relationships. Going through that relational experience has taught me that my words really can bring death or life.

> The tongue that heals is a tree of life,
>
> but a devious tongue breaks the spirit.
>
> Prov. 15:4

Every day we have the opportunity to speak words of life to others. In fact, more and more research is revealing that when a person uses their words positively with another person, "happy" chemicals release in the brain of not only the recipient, but also the one delivering the life-giving words!

In a Bible study that I have been doing recently, we were asked to write a letter to our closest relationship, expressing qualities that we love about that person. Since my husband, Stu, is that person for me, I wrote to him. As I wrote this note, I was convicted of how long it had been since I had spoken some of these things . . . ways I love him and qualities I admire in him. His reaction to this note was so sweet, and I was blessed by knowing I had touched his heart by this simple gesture.

Take a look around. Is there someone who needs some encouragement? Is there a person who needs to know how much they mean to you? Are there words of healing that need to take place?

Let me encourage you today. Do it. Say the life-giving words. After all, *your mouth matters!* ◆

DENISE'S PRACTICAL IDEAS FOR USING YOUR WORDS TO EDIFY OTHERS

Text them words of Scripture when you know they are going through something and they need to hear some encouragement. Or better yet, write them a note. Who doesn't *love* getting a handwritten note in the mail?

When you think of someone that you are blessed by, say it. Don't just think it. Call them and let them know. Why are we so reluctant to just say those things? Don't wait till it's too late.

"LET YOUR SPEECH

ALWAYS BE GRACIOUS,

SEASONED WITH SALT, SO

THAT YOU MAY KNOW HOW YOU

SHOULD ANSWER EACH PERSON."

COLOSSIANS 4:6 CSB

Be intentionally aware of the moments when those you love do something kind or well. Say it verbally to them that you noticed something positive that they did. (As a parent I'm so quick to mention the negative things I see, so why can't I verbally notice the positive things as often? Intentionality is the key!)

People need hugs. We've gotten away from giving out hugs to those we love.

Listen to this wonderful message on the power of words by Shawna Keller: relayoftruth.com/podcast/2019/2/13/wisdom-our-mouths-matter.

Share a time your words had a profound impact in a certain situation.

What wisdom did you glean from this experience that you could pass on to someone else?

HOSPITALITY

Everything I know about hospitality, I learned from my mom. When I was growing up, she truly loved (and still does!) having people in our home, and you could always count on her to have an overabundance of "good eats" for all who entered our doors. Making others feel loved and welcome is one of her finest traits! I would even call it a spiritual gift.

The Bible speaks often of welcoming guests and even "strangers" into our home with arms wide open—taking care of people with nothing expected in return. It is so rewarding to set aside a day (or an hour!) to prepare something special and invite others to enjoy it.

Yet, as I look around these days, I believe the art of hospitality is slowly becoming something it was never meant to be. With the pressure to make a meal "Instagram worthy" and a table setting that is "Pinterest perfect," lots of times it just seems easier to do nothing at all. But hospitality isn't about perfection, is it? It's about *people*! It's about having those you love into your home to feed them and love them with whatever you have the means to offer, and not being anxious about what you perceive that you lack.

The truth is, our time is our most valuable asset, and when you choose to give it to others, it shows them a kind of sacrificial love. Nothing is better than this—not even the most expertly prepared filet mignon! True hospitality brings with it what we all want—human connection!

They say the way to a man's heart is through his stomach, but I think the way to *anyone's* heart is through their stomach. This is why I have included a most beloved recipe in this very book—so now you have no excuse not to invite loved ones around you for a simple and meaningful time together. I hope these words are a challenge to fling wide open the doors of our homes, to the saints, sinners, and sojourners alike, and get our kitchens and conversations cookin'! ◆

Don't neglect to show hospitality, for by doing this
some have welcomed angels as guests without knowing it.
Heb. 13:2

MOM'S ISLAND RICE SALAD

This is a great recipe to bring to a big cookout or family gathering.
It makes a very large amount!

RICE MIXTURE

2 cups basmati rice, cooked according to package directions

1/2 cup golden raisins

1/2 cup dried cranberries

1/2 cup dried crushed banana chips

1/4 cup diced red onion

3 green onions, thinly sliced, white and green parts

1/3 cup toasted sliced almonds

DRESSING

1/4 cup red wine vinegar

1 heaping tablespoon of curry powder

2 teaspoons cumin

2 teaspoons finely chopped garlic

1/3 cup honey

1/2 cup light olive oil

fresh ground pepper

salt to taste

INSTRUCTIONS

1. Cook basmati rice according to package directions, drain, then rinse well with cold water. Add the rest of the Rice Mixture ingredients.
2. Whisk all Dressing ingredients together, and then stir into Rice Mixture. Adjust salt and pepper to taste.

"HOSPITALITY ISN'T ABOUT PERFECTION. IT'S ABOUT PEOPLE."

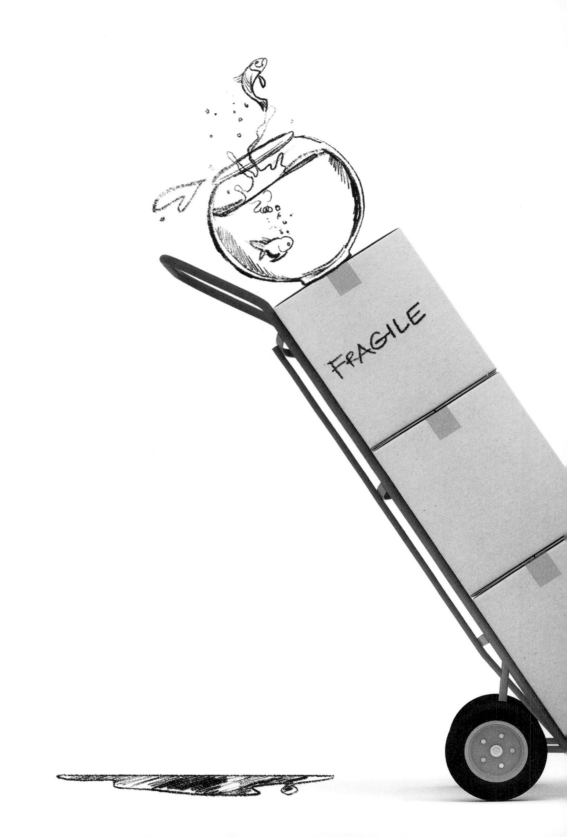

MOVING

When my husband Dana and I moved out of our apartment into our first home, we were so excited. The anticipation of the adventure ahead brought utter joy! Since we had only been married about five years and lived very simply, the amount of boxes and furniture was quite manageable.

Then four years later, we moved to what we thought would be our "forever" home. We picked out the colors, the backsplash, and even a few design elements. In our mind, we were *never* leaving! But then the unexpected 2008 recession hit and changed our minds. We considered it wise to take advantage of the market, sell the home we were *never* going to leave and move into a home we *never* even dreamed of having.

Talk about emotions. The house we were moving from held unforgettable memories—bringing our baby girl home from the hospital, warm holiday traditions, and foundational moments for our family. We didn't want to leave those things.

Eventually we did have to move on, though, and the next home somehow surpassed the experience of the last. We ended up moving into the same neighborhood as some of our closest friends, and that season of life gave us precious memories, fantastic fellowship, and best of all, a brand-new baby boy who arrived on Thanksgiving 2012! I thank God for every moment we were privileged to call that house our home.

You'd think we'd be done moving at this point, right? Nope. After seven years in that home, we yet again moved for financial reasons—to use the profits to help us become debt-free. We knew this was what we needed to do . . . but our hearts had a tougher time letting go this time around. It wasn't just the house—it was the deep *relationships* that would not be as accessible, and we had to mourn those.

What I have learned in these twenty-seven years regarding the process of moving is very simple: give yourself the permission and time to be emotionally impacted, as well as physically, mentally, and spiritually. As Ecclesiastes 3:4 says, there's "a time to weep and a time to laugh; a time to mourn and a time to dance." Give yourself a time to weep, laugh, mourn, and dance around a place God gave you to call home. Doing all of these things—without shame or guilt—is vital to the process of really dealing with a move in a healthy way.

Whether the move is a happy time for you, or a bit more disappointing, being honest with God about how you're doing—emotionally, physically, mentally, and spiritually—will keep your heart settled. ◆

"IN EVERY WAY IMAGINABLE, HE IS ABLE TO SEE US THROUGH THE INTENSE TRANSITIONS OF LIFE."

LEIGH'S TIPS ON PROCESSING A MOVE

1 PHYSICALLY

You need to *declutter*. Otherwise you or someone will have to *move it*, *unwrap it*, or *fix it*. Decluttering changes the literal, physical space around you, as well as your experience within it. To do this, start in the closets and then go room by room. This process will keep you from being overwhelmed.

And remember, we think more clearly when we are not bogged down with so much *stuff*! There's a reason Jesus tells us to give our things away. Yes, to test if they matter to us more than Him, but also because it's *actually good for us* not to be so burdened with material possessions. Purging our things can lift the heavy excess out of our spirits as much as our homes. Have yard sales, donate to people or organizations, and be sure you actually *need* (not just *want*) the items you keep. Keep in mind that the world as we know it is not our final home, and we can't take it with us. If you don't need it, someone else just might.

2 MENTALLY

When it comes to smarts, the big strategy here is buying within your budget. This is key because it promotes less stress, which equals more peace. Owning a home is similar to having a baby: they always need something, and if you have strangled yourself financially, you have no flexibility or freedom to meet the need that arises. Buy the home that suits your needs and not your wishes.

3 SPIRITUALLY

This category will sustain you through all of the above because God is able to meet us in our physical experiences, emotional moments, and even in our minds. In every way imaginable, He is able to see us through the intense transitions of life. This last move exercised my faith and trust in the Lord more strenuously than ever before.

Practically speaking, the best way to accept the change that God is bringing, especially with a move, is to dig in with both feet once you're in a new place. Saying "yes" to God in this new season means getting to know your neighbors in a deeply relational way; this is very important. God's work in the hearts of those near you usually starts with a relationship. Taking time to interact with your neighbors can change lives! Ask God for those opportunities. He won't let you down. And don't forget to pray God's blessings over your home. Ask Him to use it as He sees fit and watch your house become home sweet home for not only your family, but a warm place of fellowship for your local church and even spiritual seekers within your spheres of influence.

What has God taught you about the transitional time of moving?

What advice could you pass on to someone else who might be braving this experience right now?

SWEEPING THINGS UNDER THE RUG

Housekeeping has never been my favorite pastime. As a child, my mom and I probably argued more about cleaning my room than anything else. There isn't anything I enjoy about it. Some people think it's therapeutic. Not me. I want to get it done as quickly as possible and move on to the things that I enjoy. However, I have learned the hard way, that when we just "get by" and shove things in the closet or under the bed, the junk builds up.

The same goes for our personal lives as well, doesn't it? My marriage is better today than ever, but a few years back we had to undergo a massive overhaul. The junk had been swept under the rug for too long. I was the first Point of Grace woman to be married at the very beginning of our career. My husband, Stu, has been nothing but amazingly supportive of me from the very beginning—almost to the detriment of himself.

Stu suffered from an undiagnosed sleep disorder for *years*. We always chalked it up to strange hours at the ER (he's a Physician Assistant) and a type-A personality. Going without quality and consistent sleep for long amounts of time wreaks havoc on the body. I began to see the signs, but I knew if I addressed the issue, I might have to consider things like taking time off or leaving the group, and if I'm honest, I just didn't want to.

Stu pushed himself to always be "on" for our boys and me, but things were beginning to slide and it was obvious he wasn't well. It all came to a head when he got so sick that we ended up in an ER not knowing what was ahead.

This moment in our family life was a wake-up call to me. How could I have refused to work through some of the "not so fun things" in life just because it might take some effort or sacrifice? Why couldn't I lay down something I enjoyed for something as important as his health? Now, I had no choice. Thankfully our community group at church, Shelley, Leigh, and our pastors helped us clean up our mess together. I will forever be indebted to those friends who held us together, made us meals, and sat with us through some really dark days.

That moment in my life forever changed me. I have experienced grace and redemption in my life through God's healing power in a way I never will forget. I won't say my house-cleaning skills have gotten better, but when it comes to relationships, I've learned a lot. I've learned to bring all that junk building up under the rug out into the light where it can get sorted out, and I'm better for it. And you will be to, as you start dealing with what's under the rug in your own life. Let me tell you: it's okay if you need a few friends to help. Just know God's amazing grace will meet you no matter how big the mess. As one of our songs says, "There's Nothing Greater than His Grace!" ◆

"If we do not deal with the issues in our lives, those issues will eventually deal with us."

NANCY ALCORN
my friend and founder and president of Mercy Multiplied

"God's amazing grace will meet you no matter how big the mess."

What might you be hiding under the rug?

What have you shoved in the back closet that is piling up so high it could tip over at any moment?

What did you learn from this experience?

What wisdom would you pass on to someone who is afraid to deal with their own mess that is building up?

MARRIAGE

The Point of Grace girls and I have a lot of similarities in our upbringing. We all have only sisters, we are all from the South, and, the favorite of our commonalities, we each had an amazing example of marriage to grow up watching. All three sets of our parents have been married more than fifty years each—what an amazing testimony of commitment!

It is not lost on me what a rare and special gift this is. Certainly, there were times of crisis, of discontent, and hosts of other issues that life threw their way—but through it all, they stuck together. And that's the beauty of long-term dedication. What an amazing legacy to leave for your children.

There is no way anyone can possibly know what they are signing up for when they head to the altar. I certainly didn't, and if you are married,

I bet you can say the same. Marriage for David and me has fortunately been really great for most of the twenty-three years we have shared. Have we had some trying times? Absolutely. Have we both been in tears on the couch of a counselor's office a time or two in defense of our marriage? You bet we have. Here's the thing—it's all part of the bigger story God is writing in each of our lives. The inevitability of trying times in a marriage should be a given when you say, "I do." Huge, life-changing problems *will* come your way—and to weather them together is sanctification in one of its purest forms.

I love the phrase "weather together" because it reminds me of how I look at marriage as I get older, and even life itself. The word *weather* always brings to mind the changing of the seasons—and that is how I look back on my twenty-three years

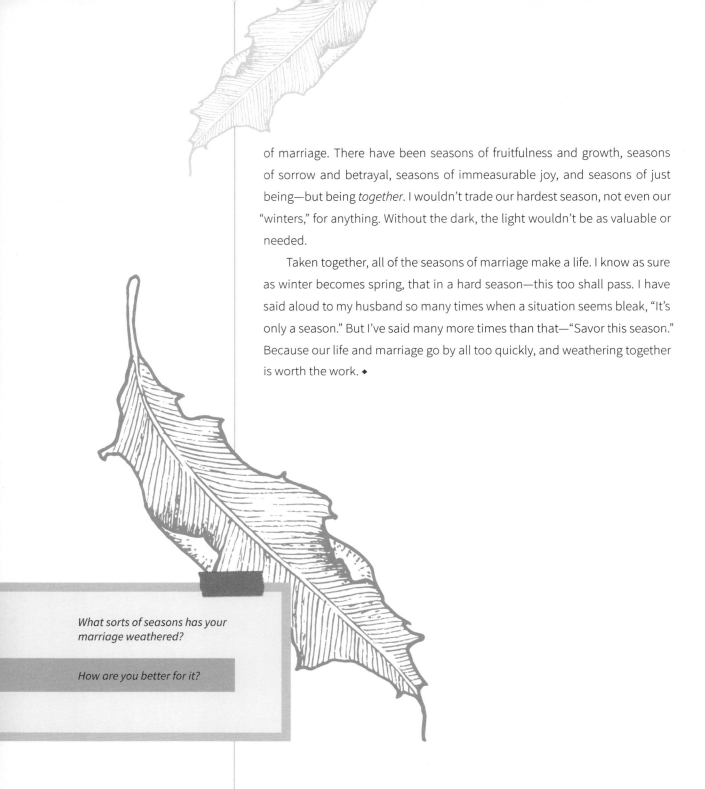

of marriage. There have been seasons of fruitfulness and growth, seasons of sorrow and betrayal, seasons of immeasurable joy, and seasons of just being—but being *together*. I wouldn't trade our hardest season, not even our "winters," for anything. Without the dark, the light wouldn't be as valuable or needed.

Taken together, all of the seasons of marriage make a life. I know as sure as winter becomes spring, that in a hard season—this too shall pass. I have said aloud to my husband so many times when a situation seems bleak, "It's only a season." But I've said many more times than that—"Savor this season." Because our life and marriage go by all too quickly, and weathering together is worth the work. ◆

What sorts of seasons has your marriage weathered?

How are you better for it?

"WEATHERING TOGETHER IS WORTH THE WORK."

STRESS

I don't know anyone, especially any woman, who would say she doesn't ever experience some sort of stress. Sometimes we bring it on ourselves, and other times, life just happens.

If there is something I've noticed as I've grown older, it's that overcommitting myself has brought about a lot of unnecessary stress. When God tells us in Proverbs 16:3 to "commit your activities to the Lord," He isn't just saying to fill up your calendar and then ask Him to be with you throughout the day. He is saying He wants us to approach Him with the opportunities we have, and let *Him* help us choose what is most purposeful. That way we aren't drowning in commitments that God never called us to.

However, it's the worries that keep us up at night and send our thoughts spinning out of control. And yet, here is the hard truth. Over and over again, the Bible commands us—*do not be anxious, do not be afraid, and do not worry about tomorrow*—whether we can control the source of stress in our life or not.

As the saying goes, "Anxiety is just calculating our future without God." How many hours a day do I try to predict what might happen? When we don't put God in our future, then yes, our worries about our kids, finances, marriage, weight, college tuition, and so on, often seem hopeless. But with God, who holds our future in His hands, there is hope! After all, He is the God of the unknown. What is unknown to me is known to Him, and I can rest in that.

What can we do in the stressed-out moments? One of the best tools I've learned through a Bible

Record some instances where you trusted God with your worries and fears instead of trusting yourself with them, and share how God moved in these circumstances.

study I'm doing is to have an Anxiety Box. When those things begin to enter my mind, I write them on a piece of paper, put them in the box, and tell God that I'm going to let Him have that problem. It's my way of obeying 1 Peter 5:7: "casting all your anxieties on him, because he cares for you" (ESV).

I may have to put those slips of paper in again and again for the same issues, but when I acknowledge that God is in control and knows how the game ends, then slowly I become less stressed. It's truly amazing when I've looked back into that box a year later and have seen how many of those things I was worried about never even happened! It renews my faith to see how God took care of me throughout whatever situation I was dealing with. And the same is true for you. God will take care of you during the stressors of life, and with Him in your future, there is always hope. ◆

"I'm a recovering 'forecaster,' and God has been so patient and kind with me as He has helped me to loosen my grip on the 'what-ifs' that can paralyze us as moms. Two beautiful ways He has taught me how to battle those times are with me speaking His Scriptures out loud over what's troubling me and by me going to my 'thankful place'—literally making myself sit down and write a list of things I'm thankful for at the moment. His peace invades my mind and seems to take over those 'what-ifs.'"

KELLY BERRY
my dear friend who has walked life just a little bit ahead of me and children's book author of Sugar Pie's Shoes *and* The Tasty Thumb

"Anxiety

HOW TO BUILD
YOUR OWN ANXIETY BOX

Find a decorative box that can be pretty enough to be kept out on a table by your bed or where you read your Bible. You can pick one up at a store or make it yourself!

Put a small notebook and pen inside the box.

When you are struggling with an issue that you are anxious about and keep wanting to hold on to it, rehash it, or dwell on it, write the issue on the paper, pray to the Lord, and put it in the box. This is a symbol of you giving that issue over to the Lord. Sometimes you may have to write it again and again, but the act of handing it over is a physical sign to your heart and mind of giving your burden to God. Let Him take it off your shoulders.

is calculating our future without God."

REGRETS AND GRACE

I grew up in a wonderful Christian home where I was involved in many wonderful things—VBS, youth choir, Bible studies, and more.

As I got older and began dating, things started to change. I gave more time and attention to boys than protecting my relationship with Jesus and His Word. I didn't realize how important it was for God to have true authority in all of my relationships, especially when it came to boyfriends.

In a particularly insecure season during college, I got involved in a sexual relationship, even though I knew somewhere in my head this wasn't God's plan for me. In many moments of weakness, I crossed lines I wanted to cross in the moment, but knew were wrong in my heart. I let my emotions make my choices—choices that would scar me for life.

Just after my nineteenth birthday I found out I was pregnant, and I had an abortion. Similar to my experience with sexual sin, I knew the right thing to do, but let my fearful emotions make my choices instead of the Lord. I didn't have the courage to face the process of pregnancy, birth, and young motherhood—things I knew the Lord could empower me in and see me through—so I took the easy, yet lethal way out. This experience brought with it the most intense shame and guilt I have *ever* felt.

I never thought in a million years that this would be part of my story. No one does. Through all the secrets and hiding of my sin, God sent so many messengers to me about His love, His gospel, and His forgiveness. Eventually, I acknowledged my sin to Jesus and others. I confessed that what I did was wrong—something so many women don't do for fear of what others will think. The Lord helped me see that yes, my decision was wrong, but it was thankfully not unforgivable. His death on the cross was the payment required by God for all sin, every sin, *even this hidden, horrible, heavy sin of mine*! That's real love!

It was God's love and kindness in this very situation that brought me into a real relationship with Him. I finally understood His unconditional love for wretched sinners and hiders like me. My story is my story and you have your story, but God wants all of us to have His forgiveness and His power so we can make better choices—choices informed by Him and His Word, not our faulty perspective or emotions. When we obey what He wants instead of what we want, we can live in protection and peace! No regrets!

I am living proof of God's mercy and grace. I'm not sure where you stand but if you are like me, bearing a hidden scar from your past, let my story be a reminder of what Christ did on the cross for each of us. He bore our scars, our sins, and He washed us white as snow. Remember that. No matter what you hide, if you come to Him with it, and surrender and believe in what He's done for you in the gospel, you can be white as snow. ◆

"THOUGH YOUR SINS ARE SCARLET,

THEY WILL BE AS WHITE AS SNOW."

ISAIAH 1:18 CSB

Do you have any hidden scars?

What holds you back from being honest with God about them?

What do you need to do in order to overcome this barrier and enjoy the forgiveness and love offered to you in the gospel?

What has God taught you over the years about your own past regrets? What advice would you pass on to others about this?

BOUNDARIES

With the dawn of social media, have you noticed that people we typically would have lost touch with years ago are back in our lives and, for better or worse, in our headspace? While we may have more "relationships" overall, I believe we also have far fewer meaningful ones. It seems we have taken the time, effort, and energy we once invested in a few deep, real-life relationships, and redirected these things toward shallow, quick touches with all the people in all the online places. We forget that Ephesians 5:15–16 tells us to "Pay careful attention, then, to how you walk—not as unwise people but as wise—making the most of the time . . ."

Sometimes it's hard to remember that the community God has placed physically right next to us deserves the majority of our time and attention. Screen time with online people makes us miss out on so much ministry and friendship that could happen, literally, right next door to us! And it's not only the people that inhabit our screen space; we have more and more people every day that inhabit our real-life space too. New connections with others are being formed constantly as we live our lives, and I have learned the hard way that we simply can't have as many relationships as we think we can, especially if we want to care for and nurture them as we should. If you are a "people-pleaser" like me, then you know exactly what I mean.

One way I have tried to set healthy relational boundaries and invest in the people right in front of me is to think of my relationships almost like concentric circles. Each circle is a boundary or line of protection around what is inside of it. If things are okay in the central circle with God and my immediate family, I can move outward to the next circle, which would be my extended family. If your relatives live far away, you know this is sometimes a challenge, but planning regular phone calls and visits is truly so important. My sister Robyn and I go through seasons where we are very good about picking up the phone and catching up, and seasons where we are both busy and not so good about it. The point is—it's important to think about and cherish the

relationships in that circle. And if my family is tended to, I can then move outward again to our (literal) neighbors and friends in my close community at church and school, and so it goes. This is a loose way of thinking about boundaries, but I have found it helpful.

This sort of paradigm helps me navigate the random requests for my time. For example, I just got a text from an old business friend who wanted to get coffee and catch up while he was in town for a few days. As much as I wanted to go, and though I could have said yes, I respectfully declined his invitation. Why? Because one of my circles needed attention, and the time I would have given away to someone that I love but am not super close to, needed to be given to someone in my family.

I'll leave you with this: Jesus had only twelve disciples that He spent the majority of His time with. And of the twelve, He had three that were closest to Him—Peter, James, and John. If Jesus Himself had only twelve very close relationships, why should we assume we can handle so many more in our own lives? It seems He set healthy boundaries. Shouldn't we?

While your circles might look different from mine, they matter. Ask the Lord to help you prioritize and nurture the relationships that you are meant to have, and then invest your time and attention accordingly. There is so much richness that is added to our lives when we are fully invested where we are supposed to be! ◆

"Boundaries are needed in all types of relationships. For me, boundaries within the parenting relationship have been the most challenging—and also the most rewarding—of all. My parenting boundaries have changed through the years. As the mother of grown and married sons, my role is less 'shaping and directing' and more 'silence, encouragement, and prayer.' As a parent, after so many years of shepherding our kids directly, the 'stepping back' can be challenging as they make their own way in the world. But we should always pray their Father's blessing over them as they marry and have their own children, believing that they were and are a gift from God for our lifetime."

COOKIE NEWTON
my friend

What has God taught you about relational boundaries?

What advice would you pass on to family members or friends about investing their energy well in the people that matter most?

What practical advice would you give them as they fight against the things that keep them from the wisest use of their time and attention?

"PAY CAREFUL ATTENTION, THEN, TO HOW YOU WALK — NOT AS UNWISE PEOPLE BUT AS WISE — MAKING THE MOST OF THE TIME..."

EPHESIANS 5:15–16 CSB

TECHNOLOGY

FAST

Last fall, my church had a forty-day season of prayer and fasting. Our leaders provided us with daily Scripture and outlines for prayer while encouraging us to fast from food or anything else that we felt led to abstain from during our time. I decided to take those forty days to fast from social media.

Could I do it? How in the world could I live without knowing what was happening in the lives of people around me? What they are eating for lunch, where they are going on vacation, what new recipe they are making for dinner? Yes, I'm exaggerating, but honestly, the process was really good for me. I didn't recognize how many times I'd picked up my phone and instantly gone to my social media outlets. It took a week to stop the habit of picking up my phone every moment I had some downtime.

I found that there were actual moments in my day I would just sit and breathe instead of immediately picking up my phone while waiting for an appointment or

even, embarrassingly enough, sitting at a stoplight. I had moments to think, to pray, to process. Time moved a little slower, and it was nice.

I don't know what your relationship with your devices is like on a daily basis, but if you find yourself needing to engage with it in every spare moment like I did, I would encourage you to consider taking a break every once in a while. You might find yourself feeling a little less stressed and realizing it's nice not knowing everyone's business all of the time. For me, even after the fast ended, my old go-to habit of looking at my social feeds during my spare time lost its charm. The pull wasn't as strong. It just didn't seem as important.

Psalm 46:10 says, "Be still, and know that I am God" (ESV). I think God put this in the Bible because He knows how tempted we are to fill our minds and days with busy, busy, busy. Fasting from technology is an easy way to put this command into practice, and enjoy the rest and calm that comes with it. ◆

In what ways has technology filled your spare moments?

How do you think this is affecting you? Your friendships? Your family?

If not technology, is there another area of your life where God is asking you to be still?

What advice would you share with those you love about what you've learned, and how to honor God in a tech-oriented world?

DENISE'S IDEAS FOR PRACTICING MODERATION WITH TECHNOLOGY AFTER THE FAST IS OVER

At dinner, no one in the family can use their phones.

Kids' phones have to be shut off at a certain time every night.

Resist looking at my social media apps before I've had time to sit and read my Bible. We are always saying, "I'm just so busy I don't have time to do my Bible study." But how many minutes did I sit and scroll through social media today?

Certain states have adopted laws that ban using your phone while driving. The new law in my own state has helped me not look at my phone while in the car. Now it always stays in my purse!

Take a walk without bringing a phone or device.

"Be still, and know that I am God."

PSALM 46:10 ESV

LISTENING

"Let me see your eyes."
"Let's turn our ears on and zip our mouths."

I've said these phrases often to my Sunday school class of little three-year-olds. It's a challenge for many of us to shut our mouths and actually listen to someone without wanting to interrupt or offer some advice.

We see this in the case of Job conversing with three friends who had *much* to say about his pain. They were pretty good about sitting quietly for a moment, but then they all had important opinions they just *had* to share, and in the end, they probably should have stayed silent for just a little bit longer because their opinions weren't exactly spot-on.

As it turns out, just like the three-year-olds and Job's friends, we all need to turn our ears on and zip our lips to really see, hear, and take to heart what those around us may be going through. How often am I willing to just sit and *be* with someone in their pain? Not say a word? Not try to fix something for them? It's hard to do. The art of listening takes practice.

We've all heard it said, "God gave us two ears and one mouth." The reason that phrase has circulated so well is because it's so true. What if I were to actually let my husband tell me about his day without chiming in on how I would fix something at the office? What if I let my children tell me what happened at school without immediately offering up what I think they should have said or what *I'm* going to do to solve the problem? Or, what if I let a friend share how she's been hurt and simply cried with her instead of strategizing a way to bring the cavalry in?

James 1:19 says we should be "quick to listen" and "slow to speak." To obey this, I've had to regularly ask the Holy Spirit to awaken my ears in awareness of those moments I simply need to be quiet. He has been faithful to help me with this. I don't do it perfectly every chance I get, but I am a work in progress. Thankfully the Lord is patient with me, and He will be with you too as you trust Him when it's time to turn on your ears and zip your mouth. ◆

One of my dear friends, Michelle, is a coach and counselor for young teen girls and women. She taught me an important lesson in listening—always parent with the "No Shock Face." No matter what they tell you, you must keep a calm and straight face as you listen. She also passes on this wisdom as you seek to listen to others:

"When there comes a moment to share advice, instead ask clarifying questions. Open-ended heart questions. Jesus Himself asked powerful questions quite often when He could have given answers. This space-holding, eyes-locked, soul-connecting, active listening is the greatest gift you can give another person."

MICHELLE DOLAN
my friend and Certified Life Coach for teen girls and young women

When did the practice of listening well deeply impact a certain relationship in your life?

What are some meaningful questions to ask others—questions that spur on good conversation and the art of listening?

"EVERYONE SHOULD BE QUICK TO LISTEN, SLOW TO SPEAK ..."

JAMES 1:19 CSB

ADDICTION

Addiction is no respecter of person. It comes in many forms of disguise, and it can wreak havoc on all who fall prey to its power and control. And the worst part of addiction is that it affects more than *just* the addict. Its destruction spills onto everyone the addict loves. My family has personally seen addiction disrupt and even destroy those we hold dear.

Debbie Petersen is my dearest friend and mentor, and she certainly understands the impact of addiction on a person. With more than twenty-five years of friendship and irrefutable godly influence, Debbie has pointed me toward Scripture and guidance on this issue, and she has given me her valuable insight on the gripping power and fear of addiction.

When Debbie shared her experiences with me about growing up as the daughter of alcoholic parents, a few things stood out to me. The first was this: there's no case in which living with an alcoholic does not profoundly and adversely impact a child. Both of her parents were functioning alcoholics, though they never called it that. They were periodically drunk and would have terrible fights, sometimes violent

How have you
or loved ones
been impacted
by addiction?

How did you
handle this?

What sort of
addictions are
present in your
own life—big
or small? How
could you take
a next step in
addressing
them?

What pieces of
advice would
you offer to
others on
the topic of
addiction?

and sometimes the police were called. Doors were broken down, and both of them were abused and hurt by the other. In speaking of these situations, her mother often told her, "Don't tell your business to someone else," so all of this chaos and trauma were stuffed inside this little girl.

What stood out to me the most was Debbie's perspective on how God has worked through her to not only change *her* for the better, but also help others. Just as God took care of her in childhood, she also knows He gave her the power to lay down alcohol herself in adulthood. In her words: "I did copy my parents and became a bad drinker, repeating a lot of their behavior, but when I became a Christian at twenty-nine, I was blown away by God's changing my life. It has been thirty-eight years since I have had a drink. My best decision in life was to decide to follow Jesus and the second was to stop drinking, because the truth is, alcohol was my 'god,' and when I met Jesus, He would not share His throne. He became my audience of One and the love of my life." And the result of this work of God in Debbie's life? Godly overflow and ministry to others, especially children. As she says, "Because my pain has led me to get counseling and study the way children are affected by alcoholism, I now feel that I can speak into this dysfunction with confidence."

Debbie's best piece of advice is to encourage and not tear down the addicts that we know and love them by speaking the truth in love, as Scripture says. In her words, this means "to not be condemning, but to come alongside. I have gone with many to AA meetings or come alongside in other ways, because so many people did these things for me when I was struggling to quit drinking."

Debbie's story is an inspiring one. And truth be told, we are all like her. *All* of us have sinned and fallen short of God's glory, but because of Christ's grace and mercy for us, each of us are invited to His table. Knowing that we all have our stories—whether they be about addiction or otherwise—helps equalize our hearts with others. This is the benefit of watching God turn our ashes into beauty. ◆

"ALL OF US

HAVE SINNED AND FALLEN SHORT OF GOD'S GLORY,

BUT BECAUSE OF CHRIST'S GRACE AND MERCY

FOR US, EACH OF US ARE INVITED TO HIS TABLE."

HEALTH AND BALANCE

It's taken me a long time to get comfortable with my health. I've done CrossFit, had a personal trainer, and even done aerobics (a *long* time ago). I've stopped eating gluten, tried no-carb, and worked on intermittent fasting and all sorts of other plans. All of these things in the name of health. What does it mean to be "healthy" anyway?

I'm really trying to learn the importance of being balanced. It's hard. Every single thing we see says we should be skinnier, younger-looking, super women. We should focus on the outside. But how much time, effort, and brain energy does it take to look like that? And let's face it. Most of us will never look like what we see in advertisements.

There has to be a balance. Exercise is super important for lots of reasons, one being that the Bible tells us to steward our bodies well, as they are His temple (1 Cor. 6:19). Also there's the common sense reasons of quality of life, mental health, and physical wellness. But the Bible also says that while the world looks at the outer appearance of a person, God looks at the heart (1 Sam. 16:7). He praises the woman who fears the Lord (Prov. 31:30). A woman's character is her adornment (Prov. 31:25; 1 Pet. 3:4). It even goes on to say that the training of the body has a limited benefit, whereas developing your godliness lasts forever (1 Tim. 4:8). I think about the years I've spent with exercise and diets. Where would I be now if I had put just as much effort into building my faith and character muscles?

At the end of the day, I just know that there are more important things in life than having the perfect body. I have to remind myself of that often. Think about the women who've meant the most to you in your life. Why? Because they are attractive

> " **For the training of the body has limited benefit, but godliness is beneficial in every way, since it holds promise for the present life and also for the life to come.**"
>
> 1 Timothy 4:8 CSB

and skinny in the world's eyes? *Or* is it someone who has loved you and cared about you the most? I want my kids to one day say, "My mom was active and beautiful because she loved God and it showed up in the way she cared for me and spent time with me and taught me how to be a healthy person," not "My mom was always at the gym because she only cared about her body." This begs the question: What are we investing our time in? What type of muscles are you building? What is your motive for being healthy?

Exercise and eating well are parts of our walk in obedience. As I mentioned before, God says to take care of our temple. It's the only one we have, but He doesn't say to obsess over our temple. So how can we balance these things? How can we be the women who take care of our own bodies so that we can love others well?

I've found that we can blend some of these together in a way that takes care of our outer self and our inner self at the same time, and keeps our motives in check. Here are some ideas: While you walk, pray. Fast sometimes, but fill yourself with God's Word too. Relax and sit in the quiet presence of God. Maybe dance around the house to praise and worship music while no one else is watching. Spend as much time investing spiritually in yourself and others as you do in your exercise time. Lift weights or resistance bands while you memorize Scripture. Eat while you remember the God who sustains you.

While these ideas are certainly not exhaustive, and I definitely haven't done them perfectly in every season, I've found that they can help you remember God, strike a good balance in your life, and be healthy for the right reasons. ◆

that Da Vinci himself painted it, not some imposter. As soon as I read the definition I thought to myself, *Well, that essay just wrote itself, didn't it?*

If you are a Christ-follower, these three words should give you great peace and perspective of undisputed origin. We don't have to work hard to "be" authentic, we already *are* by sheer definition. We originated in God. He is our Creator. And on top of that, our origin of relationship with Him is also found within the purchase price by which we were bought and redeemed. The beginning of our new life in Christ started on the cross and that informs everything else about us. History tells us that day, where that purchase was made, is undisputed. As for "our truth"? Our truth is Christ's truth—and we are inseparable from it!

The takeaway here is that we only need to be who we *already are* according to God to be truly authentic. What a relief! We come from an undisputed origin—God Himself. And if that wasn't enough, we have been reconciled to Him through the cross of Christ. Friend, *this is who we are.* God is our undisputed and unchangeable beginning, and as long as we walk in Him, we are living authentic lives. ◆

"I heard my mother whistle a lot . . . and I watched her live an authentic Christian life as she went about each day, full of joy and peace, trusting God in every circumstance. I want to be like her in so many ways. The longer I live, the more I cherish the blessing of being myself before the Lord, as my mother was, and walking close to Him."

JANE HOWARD
my friend

What has God taught you about authenticity? What lies has He dispelled?

What new insights has He given you?

What advice would you pass on to others about this?

"As long as we walk in Him, we are living authentic lives."

SIBLINGS

As young as five years old, I remember singing with a trio of girls. Long before I was in Point of Grace, I was "performing" with my two older sisters, Dana (two years older) and Reide (eleven months older). My mom was the pianist and the children/youth choir director of our small country church. If we didn't have a special guest performing at our fifth Sunday night concerts, then my mom would make us girls get up and sing. (God apparently knew I would need the practice in a girls' trio!)

Growing up, I shared a room with Reide. I was the neat freak, and she was the pigpen. The three of us were normal siblings; we fought a lot, did everything together, and always had a playmate. We shared a lot of the same things, like clothes, hobbies, and one bathroom. Dana was the peacemaker and our protector, and Reide was super-smart but loved to roughhouse with me. And I was the baby . . . which obviously means the tattletale and the brat. When we weren't in trouble, we had a wonderful childhood. Having two sisters taught me to share, to compromise, to forgive, to support, and to love in a unique way.

Once my oldest sister went off to college, there was a shift in our household dynamic, and then more shifts as we each graduated college and eventually

married—all within 2 1/2 years of each other. (My poor dad's wallet and heart took a beating!) Each of us has been married more than twenty-seven years, and each of us has a son and a daughter.

Of course this is all a snapshot. We had our seriously dysfunctional moments. We certainly weren't perfect, but we did have knowledge of the perfect Christ that our parents tried to demonstrate.

I can't imagine life without Dana and Reide. I have shared some pretty difficult things with them, and they have been a rock of grace and love. They are my best friends! My siblings have supported me in what I do and have provided godly counsel when I needed it. Sisterhood is *priceless*!

Whether your "sibling" relationships come in the form of biological siblings, church friends, or a local sisterhood/brotherhood of some sort, they are gifts from God, and they are worth nurturing and protecting. You have to be intentional about keeping those relationships healthy. After all, they are the people who stick with us when life gets hard! Anything worth having takes dedication. Find a sister if you don't have one, and be a sister to someone who needs one. There is always room for another sibling in someone's family, and you might be exactly the rock they need. ◆

What are the "sibling relationships" in your life?

What have you done in the past to nurture or protect them? What do you sense you should do in these relationships to keep them healthy?

Who could you be a "sibling" to in this season of life?

What has God taught you over the years about sibling relationships? What advice would you pass down to someone else about your experience?

"FIND A SISTER IF YOU DON'T HAVE ONE, AND BE A SISTER TO SOMEONE WHO NEEDS ONE."

ENJOYING

YOUR TIME WITH

GOD

I celebrated my fiftieth birthday last year. It wasn't nearly the milestone I expected it to be, but it was a sweet time. We were in Florida for my son Price's last high school spring break. His baseball team had a tournament there. My oldest son, Spence, was able to fly down and spend a few days with us as well. As we sat there with our two boys who will soon be out of the house, I thought to myself, *This is the best birthday ever*.

Sitting there laughing and listening to them make fun of Stu and me while we waited on dinner, there was this sense of completeness. All of my people just there together enjoying each other. I adored the moment we had, just the four of us.

As I was lying in bed reliving that night full of food, gratitude, and absolute love for my kids, it hit me: *God feels this way about me*. He desires to just hear me laugh and talk, and He has a sincere pride for this child He created. He wants to have these moments with me, His child.

DENISE'S PRACTICAL IDEAS FOR MEETING WITH GOD

GET OUT AND TAKE A WALK (without trying to burn calories, just a nice stroll). Pray, look around at God's glory in creation.

TURN ON SOME LOUD PRAISE MUSIC and sing and even dance around while doing laundry or dishes or whatever else. (Note to self: you may want to make sure you are the only one home!)

JOURNAL YOUR PRAYERS TO GOD like you are writing a letter to Him. Don't try to filter the thoughts if they come in random statements, but just write like you are talking to Him.

LISTEN TO A SERMON OR PODCAST that will teach you God's Word. Or go to a Christian concert (like Point of Grace!).

MAKE SURE YOU SCHEDULE TIME IN YOUR CALENDAR to turn off the phone and find a favorite place (screen porch, favorite chair, etc.) to get a favorite drink and make time to read His Word.

His love for me is deeper, wider, longer, and higher than I can truly imagine, but I can get a little glimpse of it from this experience I had with my own family. He is mine and I am His. The same is true for you. You are loved more than you can ever imagine.

Don't let the enemy tell you that God is ashamed of you, or that you aren't worthy of His love or time, or that meeting with Him is a chore or a to-do list. These are lies. Your Father can't get enough time with you. So, carve out the time. Tell Him how much you love Him and let Him love you back. ◆

> And I pray that you, being rooted and established in love, may have power, together with all the Lord's holy people, to grasp how wide and long and high and deep is the love of Christ.
> Eph. 3:17b–18 NIV

"Throughout the years of busy life, on a day when I had little time for lengthy Bible study, I found that having a solid Christian daily devotional book gave me strength. You know, those frantic days that are unorganized, exhausting, and full of so many second pages added to your 'to-do' list. Those are the days that God has a perfect verse that calms your spirit and gives you His strength to make it through the day. It is not happenstance that a new or familiar verse is right there on the page just for you. Claim it and take it in your heart for the day. It was a gift from the Lord, and it will change how your day flows!"

BONITA SEELIG
my longtime friend and mentor

Take some time to think through the lies you believe about your time with God, and pair them with Scripture that combats these lies.

"YOUR FATHER CAN'T GET ENOUGH TIME WITH YOU."

TRUSTING GOD IN TIMES OF TROUBLE

> **"God is our refuge and strength, a helper who is always found in times of trouble."**
> **Psalm 46:1**

There's no doubt about it—times of trouble will visit all of us at one point or another. None of us gets through life without facing seasons of trial, testing, or suffering. One such season is happening as we finish up this book—the Coronavirus pandemic.

If you're anything like me (Leigh), the beginning of 2020 probably started out as usual. I got back in the gym, started the process of reading through the Bible, organized some closets, all while striving to enjoy each day to its fullest! Then March 2020 came and the world as we knew it changed dramatically!

The price of gas dropped, schools, holidays, and celebrations were cancelled everywhere, people were instructed by the government to socially distance from one another by at least six feet to stop the spread of the virus, grocery stores only let so many people in at a time (and had bare shelves when it came to toilet paper and disinfecting products), all front-line workers wore masks, entire cities were in shut-down, worldwide travel came to a halt, and no one could leave their homes apart from trips to the store for essential supplies. The Coronavirus attacked the entire world—the news was calling it a global pandemic. A "new normal" descended upon us all.

Denise: It was the most vulnerable time I've ever experienced. As we entered the time of the pandemic, we found out my husband's job was in jeopardy, and as time passed, he eventually resigned from that company. So we sat in quarantine, not knowing what our future held. One of my prayers when the pandemic began was, "God, don't let me miss what You want to show me."

TOWARD THAT END, HERE ARE SOME THINGS GOD SHOWED US DURING THE PANDEMIC:

1 Times of Trouble Give Us Perspective

Shelley: Life was moving along per the status quo before the virus swept through our nation, and I couldn't have ever imagined the situation I was about to face. Personally, I was just coming out of a season of worry (again!) about, as usual, things I cannot control—things in the future that I just knew would come to pass and bring troubles to me or my family. When the Coronavirus became a global health crisis, it changed everything. Those worries and troubles now seem so insignificant—the pandemic made every worry I once lost sleep over feel so inconsequential. And though it didn't feel comfortable to have my perspective shifted, I'm thankful for it. It has opened my eyes to what really matters.

2 Times of Trouble Pull Us Together

Leigh: There were many wonderful and unexpected side effects during the mandate to stay home during the pandemic. Our new normal forced our family into homeschooling our kids. I so enjoyed this time with my seven year old. Family time became more than people. It became a "safe" place and restored the joy of fellowship with one another. We took walks together each morning and evening. All meals were shared face-to-face—we even decided to sit at our seldom-used dining room table for each meal. We played board games instead of just seeing them stacked on a shelf. We pulled out the Wii for some old-school tennis and bowling, and I even read a book, which I rarely let myself do or have time to do!

Denise: The school shutdowns brought my boys home from college, which was definitely our biggest gift in the middle of the chaos. Who would have ever thought we would have them both home together for this amount of time? No matter what kind of suffering it may be, crisis usually brings people together, helping them return their lives to foundational relationships. Though we all mourn the ways the Coronavirus has harmed people, we also thank God for the ways He's drawn together our families and friendships, reminding us of their importance and reinforcing their bonds.

If you are facing a time of trouble right now, or know someone who is, remember to enjoy people. Love on them, reach out and make a difference today. Write letters, make the phone calls when you think of someone, take time to make someone's day. There is always someone in need, and lock-down or not, we can help meet their needs.

3 Times of Trouble Point Us to Our Future Hope

Shelley: The Coronavirus ushered in a time of immeasurable uncertainty about everything—finances, health, relationships, the future, and more. In the face of this, God has reminded me (in the most tangible way I can think of through this virus) that we have the greatest certainty of all as believers in the resurrected Christ. He battled sickness and death for us, and He won. He came out on the other side alive and well, and though we will face these things too, we will come out on the other side alive and well too. The resurrected Christ reminds us that we will one day be resurrected and made new too, and the troubles of this life—including a lethal virus—can't stop that future from happening.

4 Times of Trouble Move Us toward Prayer and Scripture

Denise: Before the pandemic hit, I don't think I realized how much I depended on other things for my sense of security. But once it did, I was reminded that my house must be built on the only thing that stands. Jesus Christ is my rock and my salvation, and His Word is where I can securely set my feet. All other ground is truly "sinking sand." To help myself stand on the one thing that wouldn't give way, I had to lean in constantly to God's Word, devotions, and messages that reminded me of God's sovereignty, goodness, and glory. These were the only things that could drive my fears of uncertainty away. I think I actually learned the meaning of praying continually!

Leigh: I quickly learned during the pandemic that "pray without ceasing" is a must, not simply a consideration. It became a true treasure of the new normal I found myself in. I prayed for our country, our president and those in authority, the victims of the virus and their families, those who lost jobs, and the front-line workers in hospitals, grocery stores, and the postal service. I also made the Lord's prayer an essential part of each day, finding assurance and provision particularly in the phrase, "give us this day our daily bread." Ultimately, prayer has been the epicenter for me during the Coronavirus outbreak. It has enlightened my eyes to new challenges, my heart toward gratitude, and a stillness of God's peace that passes my understanding.

5

Times of Trouble Are in God's Hands

Shelley: I've learned that God sustains all things and is sovereign over all things—over the world and everything that happens in it (Deut. 10:14; 2 Chron. 20:6; 1 Cor. 10:26; Heb. 1:3). Whether a global health crisis or a simple ordinary worry, our troubles are ultimately in God's hands. And what's more, He refines us through all things as we live in light of the certain things to come. I'm grateful now more than ever for that assurance.

Denise: The pandemic taught me that I am in control of nothing. We can make all of the plans we want for our future, but ultimately there are no guarantees. It's God's hands that hold everything in store for us, and though it's scary to think that our hands aren't ultimately on the wheel, it should bring us great comfort that He is the one truly in control.

As I experienced the "forced rest" of quarantine during the Coronavirus, my favorite psalm brought me comfort, revealing that there aren't more trustworthy hands we could run to in times of trouble, for He holds power over it all!

> Rest in God alone, my soul, for my hope comes from him.
> He alone is my rock and my salvation, my stronghold;
> I will not be shaken. My salvation and glory depend on God,
> my strong rock. My refuge is in God. Trust in him at all times, you people;
> pour out your hearts before him. God is our refuge.
>
> Ps. 62:5–8

What a great word for all of us in times of trouble—pandemic or otherwise! God is the refuge we can run into. He is the rock we can stand on. He is the hope we are looking for. He wants us to pour our hearts out to Him when we face something too big to handle ourselves. God is in control, and even when the whole world is reeling, we don't have to be shaken. Our God's got us. ◆

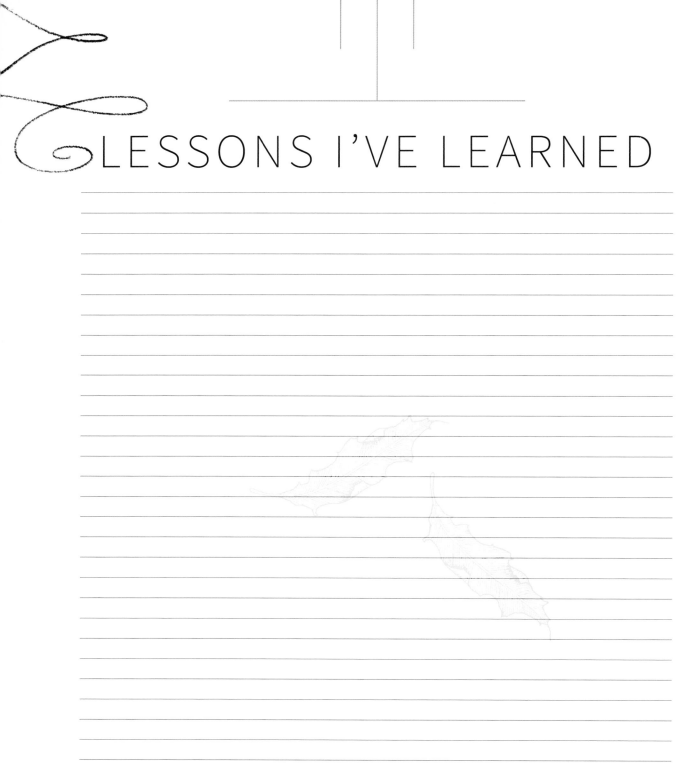

LESSONS I'VE LEARNED

To our families, thank you.

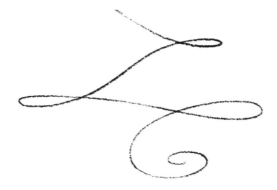